Make & Play Puppets

HANDS-ON BIBLE ACTIVITIES

FOR PRESCHOOLERS

Bonnie Temple

Group
Loveland, Colorado

Group's R.E.A.L. Guarantee to you:

Every Group resource incorporates our R.E.A.L. approach to ministry—a unique philosophy that results in long-term retention and life transformation. It's ministry that's:

This is EARL. He's R.E.A.L. mixed up. (Get it?)

Relational
Because student-to-student interaction enhances learning and builds Christian friendships.

Experiential
Because what students experience sticks with them up to 9 times longer than what they simply hear or read.

Applicable
Because the aim of Christian education is to be both hearers and doers of the Word.

Learner-based
Because students learn more and retain it longer when the process is designed according to how they learn best.

Dedication

To children in neighborhoods everywhere—may we draw them in and give them Jesus.

To the children in my neighborhood who helped me create the puppets to tell others about Jesus: Stephanie, Danielle, Cara, Shayla, Stephen, Tia, and Robert.

Make & Play Puppets: Hands-On Bible Activities for Preschoolers

Copyright © 2001 Bonnie Temple

Visit our Web site: **www.grouppublishing.com**

Credits

Editor: Linda A. Anderson
Creative Development Editor: Karl Leuthauser
Chief Creative Officer: Joani Schultz
Copy Editor: Janis Sampson
Art Directors: Andrea L. Boven and Jean Bruns
Designer: Andrea L. Boven/Boven Design Studio, Inc.
Cover Art Director: Jeff A. Storm
Computer Graphic Artist: Stephen Beer
Illustrator: Sharon Holm
Production Manager: Peggy Naylor

ISBN 0-7644-2335-5

10 9 8 7 6 5 4 3 2 1   10 09 08 07 06 05 04 03 02 01

Printed in the United States of America.

Contents

Introduction

Kids love puppets!

Preschoolers love to hold kid-size things in their hands. They love to touch, see, feel, hear, and smell as they try new things and learn about their world. This is how they learn best. So why not teach this way?

Make & Play Puppets was written to help you create memorable lessons—both meaningful and fun—for the children *and* for you! These twenty-five lessons provide a playful, age-appropriate way to teach preschoolers important Bible truths.

Whether you're intimidated by using puppets or are a pro, this book is for you because the puppeteers are the children themselves! In each session, children will make puppets using simple everyday items. Next they'll use their puppets to help tell the Bible story. Then they'll use their puppets again to respond to the story by praising God in playful, age-appropriate ways. Though the sessions are designed to enhance the storytelling of your existing curriculum, each one can also be used as a stand-alone Bible lesson.

These friendly, playful, and practical ways of making puppets from simple, hand-held items will have your preschoolers actively playing and learning important Bible truths—as easy as one, two, three!

And It Was Good!

Creation

GENESIS 1

Power Words

"God created the heavens and the earth" (Genesis 1:1).

Provisions

Before class:

• Bake chocolate chip cookie dough in a 9x13 pan.

• Cut and remove a four-inch circle from the baked cookie dough anywhere in the pan.

• Cut the rest of the cookie dough into enough bars for your class, but do not remove the bars from the pan.

• Make blue Jell-O gelatin.

• Bring a Bible to class.

For each child, you will need:

- craft sticks
- star stickers
- small sun and moon stickers
- craft feathers
- wiggly craft eyes
- glue
- Goldfish crackers
- animal crackers
- plate, spoon, napkin

Prepare It

Set the cake pan, Jell-O, a spoon, the Goldfish crackers, and the animal crackers in the story area. Set the craft sticks, stickers, feathers, craft eyes and glue on the craft table.

Gather the children around the table. Explain to them that they will make special puppets to help tell the story about God creating the heavens and the earth.

Give each child a craft stick. Have each child choose to make either a star puppet or bird puppet. To make the star puppet, place star stickers on one side of the craft stick and sun and moon stickers on the other side. To make a bird puppet, glue two feathers crosswise at the top of the stick and add eyes.

Make sure every child makes a stick puppet and that you have both stars and birds.

Proclaim It

Gather children in the story area with their star and bird puppets. Open your Bible to Genesis 1, and show it to the children.

Say: **Let's hold up our puppets for everyone to see. Such good puppets you made! We're going to use our puppets to tell our Bible story.**

In the beginning, before God made the earth, everything was dark and black. Close your eyes to make it dark. Keep them shut!

On the first day, God made the light. Open your eyes! Now you can see! God made the light so we could see.

Let's make some dark and light again. Cup your hands together and hold them tight. Now move your thumb just a little bit and peek inside. Is

it dark in there? God made the dark. Now open them up. God made the light. God made the dark and the light and it was good. Say, "It was good!"

The next thing God made was the air in the sky. Take a big gulp of fresh air. Breathe in deeply! Good job! God made the air you breathed. The air that God made was good. Say, "It was good!"

On the third day, God created the land and the sea. He was busy! Bring out the cake pan, and show it to the children. Let's pretend this cake is the earth God made. He also made the deep blue sea. Spoon some of the Jell-O into the hole in the cake. We'll pretend this blue Jell-O is the sea. The land and sea God made were good. Say, "It was good!"

Do any of you have a night light in your room at home? Well, God knew the dark was *very* dark, so he made night lights, too—they're called the stars and the moon. He also made a sun to make the day bright. If you made a star puppet, wave it in the air. Let's add those to the earth we have here. Help children stick their puppet handles into the cake. The sun, moon, and stars that God made were good. Say, "It was good!"

On the next day, the fifth day, God made the birds and fish. Let's wave the bird puppets and fly them through the air. Fly them right over to our earth cake and land them there. Help children stick their bird puppets into the earth cake. Now we need some fish. Distribute a few Goldfish crackers, and have children put the fish into the Jell-O. The fish and birds God made were good. Say, "It was good!"

Our earth cake is looking pretty busy! But we still need more. On the sixth day, God made the animals. Give each child one or two animal crackers. Let's add animals to our earth cake. Help children add animals to the cake. God did more on the sixth day. It was the best thing. It was his favorite thing of all his creation. It was people! God made the first man and woman and named them Adam and Eve. God made the animals and people and it was good. Say, "It was good!"

Our earth cake is now a beautiful creation cake! Our stars, moons, suns, and birds are in the air. The animals are down below, and the fish are in the sea. And you and I are the people! Raise your hands up in the air and say, "Thank you, God, for making me!"

Say: **When God made everything, he said, "It is good!" Let's celebrate and**

worship God for making good things. Let's have a praise parade.

Have children act out their favorite things from the creation story. They could pretend to be stars by holding up their hands and "twinkling" their fingers, move as their favorite animals move, or float like clouds. Choose an older preschooler to carry the creation cake. Lead the parade around the room. Then end the procession by having children sit in the snack area, handing back their puppets, and serving chocolate chip bars, crackers, and Jell-O.

Talk About It

Ask:

- **What are some things that God made?**
- **What's your favorite thing God made?**
- **How did God feel about what he made?**
- **How does God feel about you?**

Power Prayer

Let's wave our puppets in the air and praise God. Say, "Thank you, God, for all the good things you made. Thank you, God, for making me!" We love you, God.

God Keeps His Promises

Noah's Ark

GENESIS 6–8

"When you pass through the waters, I will be with you" (Isaiah 43:2).

Before class:

- Fill a spray bottle with water.
- Pop some popcorn.
- Set out a piece of poster board.
- Cut a three-inch slit in the center bottom of paper bowls.
- Cut crepe paper into strips about ten inches longer than the length of the poster board. Use different colors of crepe paper to represent the rainbow.
- Bring a Bible to class.

For each child, you will need:

- a crepe paper strip
- tape
- a marker
- a paper bowl with a slit in it
- a handful of popcorn
- animal stickers

 Prepare It

Set the popcorn and spray bottle in the story area. Set the markers, poster board, crepe paper strips, bowls, animal stickers, and tape on the craft table.

Gather the children around the table. Explain to them that their fingers will be special puppets to help tell a Bible story about how God keeps his promises. Give each child a paper bowl with a slit in the bottom. Have children put several animal stickers on the inside of the bowls, reminding them not to cover the slits.

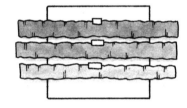

Let each child choose a crepe paper strip, and help them tape it horizontally on the poster board to make a "rainbow." If your class is large, have two children each tape an end of one strip. Center the strips so that the ends hang off the sides of the poster board.

With a marker, help each child draw a smiley face on each fingertip of one hand. (Don't include the thumb.)

Proclaim It

Gather children in the story area. Place the rainbow on the floor near you. Open your Bible to Genesis 6, and show it to the children.

Say: **Today our Bible story comes from the book of Genesis. It's about a time long ago when everyone on the earth was acting very, very bad. God could find only one man who was good. That man was Noah. Put your bowl in your lap, and hold up your index finger for Noah. Wiggle him, and say hello to Noah. Noah had three sons. Hold up your other fingers. Say hello to Noah's sons.**

Everyone else on earth was so bad that they made God sad. Show me a sad face. Then they made God mad. Show me a mad face. They would not listen to God. They would not change their ways. So God decided to send a flood to cover the whole earth.

But God promised to protect Noah and his family. **Wiggle your fingers to show that Noah was happy that God promised to protect him. He told Noah to build a great big boat called an ark.** Let's make a fist and pound on our other hand to pretend Noah and his sons are building the ark.

Good building, everyone! Then God told Noah to collect two of each animal—a mommy and a daddy—to go with him on the ark. That surprised Noah, but he was happy to do it. When the ark was finished, God said it was time to get in. Are you ready to get Noah and his family on the ark?

Show each child how to put four fingers through the slit in the bottom of the bowl. **Noah and his family got in the ark. Wiggle your fingers at me and say hi! It looks like Noah is ready, but wait—don't forget the rest of the animals!** Put a handful of popcorn into each child's boat. **That's a lot of animals! The ark is crowded. Tell Noah not to eat any of the animals while we tell his story, and make sure you wait before eating too!**

When the ark was full, the rains came. Spray the children lightly with water from the spray bottle. **It poured and poured until the whole earth was covered with water. But God kept Noah and his family safe. Move your boat and show me how Noah's ark floated on the water. Don't let any animals fall out! Now wiggle your fingers to show how happy Noah and his sons were that God protected them.**

Praise & Play With It

Say: **When the flood was over, God promised he would never ever flood the whole earth again. He put a rainbow in the sky.** Hold up the rainbow poster the children made earlier. **The rainbow was God's sign. It meant "God keeps his promises." So every time we see a rainbow, we can remember God's promise to us that he'll never again flood the whole earth. Let's praise God for keeping his promises.**

Hold the rainbow poster, and lead the children around the room as they pretend to float their arks in the water. End up at the story area. Have children pass under the rainbow, and sit down. As they pass under the rainbow, have them say, "God keeps his promises."

Say: **God always keeps his promises! Let's take our finger puppets out of the ark now and eat our popcorn. Mmm, it's good! And God is good because he always keeps his promises.**

Talk About It

Ask:

- **Did God protect Noah? In what ways?**
- **What other promise did God make?**
- **Has God promised anything to you?**
- **How does God protect you?**

3

Trouble to Triumph

Joseph

GENESIS 37–42

"We know that in all things God works for the good of those who love him" (Romans 8:28a).

Provisions

Before class:

• Cut a slit in the bottom of paper cups.

• Bring a Bible to class.

For each child, you will need:

• a white paper cup with a slit

• a flat wooden craft spoon

• markers

• pieces of different colored electrical tape

• scissors

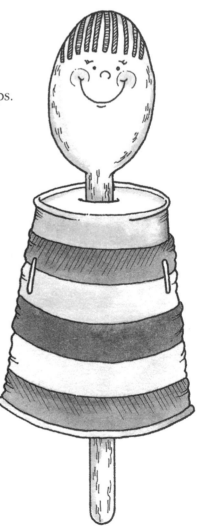

Prepare It

Set the markers, craft spoons, and paper cups with slits on the craft table. Set the electrical tape and scissors in the story area.

Gather the children around the table. Explain to them that they will make a special puppet to tell the story about a boy named Joseph.

Give each child a craft spoon, and have children each draw a face and hair on the oval end of the spoon with markers. Give them each a paper cup, and show children how to stick the spoon inside the cup and up through the slit so Joseph's head sticks up through the bottom. Show them how to use the part of the spoon inside the cup as a handle to hold the puppet. If you want, cut holes on opposite sides of each paper cup large enough to poke a finger and thumb through for puppet arms.

Proclaim It

Gather the children in the story area with their Joseph puppets. Open your Bible to Genesis 37, and show it to the children.

Say: **Our Bible story comes from the book of Genesis. Once there was a man who had twelve sons. That's a lot of kids! He loved one of his sons more than all the others. This son's name was Joseph. Hold up your puppet and say hello to Joseph.**

Because Joseph's dad loved Joseph more than his brothers, he gave him a special coat. It was colorful and fancy. Let's give Joseph his fancy coat. Cut strips of the colored electrical tape, and have children decorate their puppets with them. Then set the tape aside, and continue the story.

Show your neighbor the fancy coat you gave Joseph. Those are beautiful coats. How did Joseph feel when he got his coat? How do you think his brothers felt? Yes, they were jealous. They wanted a coat too. They were so mad at Joseph that they wanted to hurt him! They threw him into a deep pit. Bend your knees and cross your legs where you're sitting, and put your Joseph puppet in the hole your legs make.

It was deep in there, and Joseph couldn't get out. How do you think

Puppet Pointer

A large unopened can of food makes a great tape holder. Stick strips of tape around the top edge of the can, hanging off the side. Strips can be cut ahead of time, and children can pull the strips off the can without waiting for you to cut them.

15

Joseph was feeling now?

Soon some men came who were traveling to a far away country called

Praise Point

God turns trouble into good.

Egypt. Joseph's brothers sold him to the men to be their slave! Do you know what a slave is? A slave is someone who does all the hard work for someone else without getting paid. Take Joseph out of his hole now, and let's go with him to Egypt, the country where he was taken. Have kids pretend to ride donkeys, camels, or horses as they move around the room and end up in a different location.

Joseph was in a strange new place. How was Joseph feeling? He was homesick. That means he missed his home and family. But Joseph loved God. God was with Joseph and took care of him. Because Joseph forgave his brothers and did many good things in Egypt, he became a great ruler there. Because he lived there and had a good job, he saved his family from starving to death. They lived in a place where there was no food. So they came to Joseph, and he helped them. If Joseph hadn't been taken to Egypt, everyone in the family would have starved. God took Joseph's troubles and turned them into something good! That's the kind of God he is. God likes to do things like that for you and me, too!

Praise & Play With It

Say: **Sometimes we have troubles, too, just as Joseph did. Maybe sometimes you want to try things at home, but you get told that you're too little. Does that ever happen to you? Maybe there's someone older than you who is mean to you. Has that ever happened to you? Maybe someone got something special, and you didn't get anything. How did you feel when that happened?** Give a few moments for children to tell you about times when they suffered injustices.

You can be like Joseph and forgive those people. God will turn your troubles into something good. Hold your puppet up, and say as Joseph did, "God, we forgive those who hurt us."

Now turn to your neighbor, and make your puppet say to him or her, "God turns trouble into good."

Play a version of "London Bridge" by substituting the following words. When a child gets "captured," sing the words in the second stanza. Make sure each child and his or her puppet gets captured. If your group is large, have four or five kids hold hands to form the bridge, capturing several children at once. When you get to the name part in the song, sing the word "children" instead of naming the children individually.

God turns trouble into good,

Into good, into good.

God turns trouble into good.

Yes, he does!

God loves [name of child].

Yes, he does. Yes, he does. Yes, he does.

God loves [name of child].

Yes, he does. Yes, he _does_!

Talk About It

Ask:

- **What bad things happened to Joseph?**
- **What did Joseph do when his brothers were mean to him?**
- **How did God help Joseph?**
- **How can God help you?**

Power Prayer

God, help us forgive others when they hurt us. Thank you that you turn our troubles into good. We love you, Lord.

Hide and Peek

Baby Moses

EXODUS 2:1-10

Power Words

"You are my hiding place; you will protect me from trouble" (Psalm 32:7a).

Provisions

Before class:

• Cut half-inch wide elastic into lengths that are a little more than the circumference of the oval sponges. Hot glue, sew, or knot the ends of the elastic together to make a band that fits around each sponge. The elastic strap should not be so tight that it keeps the sponge from lying flat.

• Fill a plastic tub, basin, or sink with a few inches of warm water.

• Bring a Bible to class.

For each child, you will need:
- an oval sponge
- an elastic strap
- a permanent marker
- a washcloth or a piece of fabric

Prepare It

Set the tub of water and the washcloths in the story area.

Gather the children around the table. Explain to them that they will make special puppets to help tell the story of a special baby named Moses.

Give each child an oval sponge, and have children each draw eyes and a mouth at one end with a permanent marker. Show them how to slip an elastic band around the center of the sponge. They can decorate the straps and the bodies of the puppets with additional permanent markers if you want. If they do this, tell them to be careful not to get the ink on their clothing.

As they work, talk to the children about how much God loves children and babies. Then explain that today's story is about an amazing way that God took care of one special baby that was in great danger.

Proclaim It

Gather the children in the story area with their baby Moses puppets. Put the tub of water in front of you. Open your Bible to Exodus 2, and show it to the children.

Say: **Our story comes from the book of Exodus. Pharaoh was the ruler in Egypt where God's people lived. God's people were called the Hebrews. They were Pharaoh's slaves. That means they were forced to do all of Pharaoh's hard work. It was a hard time for God's people, but he loved them and blessed them and gave them big families. Soon there were so many of God's people that Pharaoh was afraid they would fight against him and take his land. So he had a wicked idea. He decided to get rid of all the Hebrew baby boys so they couldn't grow up to be big and strong and become his enemies.**

There was a Hebrew mother who had a baby boy named Moses. Show your puppet to your neighbor and say, "Hi, baby Moses." Moses' family loved him. Rock your puppet to show how you would take care of baby Moses. They fed him when he was hungry and played with him when he

was bored. Hold the strap in the back of your puppet and pretend to feed him. Then make baby Moses jump and play.

When Moses' mother heard Pharaoh's wicked plan to hurt the babies, she was very, very sad. Show me how sad she looked. But then God gave her a plan! She made a basket to hide him in, tight and warm. The basket was waterproof. That means no water could come in and get the baby wet. She wrapped him in a warm blanket, and put him in the basket. Cover your puppet with a washcloth, and give one to each child. Have them cover their puppets with the washcloths.

Then Moses' mother did a surprising thing. She took the basket and put it in the river to hide it! Place your puppet in the tub of water, and push it gently from one side to the other while you continue. She told Moses' sister, Miriam, to stay close by and see what happened.

The little basket floated down the river right to Pharaoh's palace! Miriam was worried for Moses, but God was taking care of him. Pharaoh's daughter saw the basket and peeked inside. "Oh!" she said, "There's a baby in here!" She was so happy and surprised to find the cute little baby that she decided to keep him and raise him as her own son. She asked Miriam to go find a woman to help her take care of the baby. So Miriam went and got Moses' mother!

Moses' family was so happy that he was safe and protected. God took care of Moses.

Praise & Play With It

Say: **Let's jump up and down to show how happy Moses' family was that he was safe. Wave your puppet in the air and say, "Thank you, God!" Now lay down small and quiet like baby Moses in the basket. Good job!**

Now sit up and hug baby Moses to show how much his family loved him. Have children pray, "Thank you for…" after each of the following instructions:

Let's tell God thank you for loving us.

Let's feed baby Moses. Let's thank God for giving us food.

Let's play with baby Moses. Have kids toss the puppets in the air, tickle them, and hug them. **Let's thank God for giving us playtime.**

Let's kiss baby Moses. Let's thank God for protecting us.

Let's cover baby Moses with his blanket again. Let's say, "Thank you, God, for taking care of us."

Now it's your turn to float baby Moses in the river. You can even give him a bath if you want to. There are lots of ways that God takes care of us.

Allow children to float their puppets in the water. As they play, ask them to tell you ways that God takes care of them. Encourage them to retell the story to one another. Tell them to use their puppets at home in the tub when they take a bath and to tell the story of baby Moses to their families.

Talk About It

Ask:

- **How did God take care of baby Moses?**
- **How does God take care of you?**
- **What are some ways we can thank God for taking care of us?**

Power Prayer

Thank you, God, for taking care of baby Moses. Thank you for taking care of us, too. We love you, God!

That's Amazing!

Moses and the Red Sea

EXODUS 14:10-31

"The Lord will fight for you" (Exodus 14:14a).

Before class:

• Gather an assortment of twigs and sticks from the yard for Moses' staff.

• You'll need paint stir sticks from a paint store. Stores will often donate these if you explain that they're for a preschool class.

• Bring a Bible to class.

For each child, you will need:

- a paint stir stick
- markers
- a chenille wire
- a stick or a twig
- cotton balls or fiberfill
- glue

Prepare It

Gather the children around the table. Explain to them that they will make special puppets to help tell the story about an amazing thing God did for Moses and his people.

Give each child a paint stir stick. Have them draw eyes and a nose at one end of the stick. Show them how to wrap a chenille wire around the stick, twist it once, and bring the ends back around to the front for Moses' arms and hands. Fold the tip of one of the "hands" about a quarter inch in so the sharp end isn't sticking out. Help each child wind the other "hand" around a twig to make Moses holding a staff. Help them glue fiberfill to the back of their paint sticks for hair and on the front of the sticks for beards. If you use cotton balls, gently pull them and stretch them out a little bit.

Proclaim It

Gather the children in the story area with their Moses puppets. Open your Bible to Exodus 14, and show it to the children.

Say: **Our Bible story comes from the book of Exodus. When Moses was a baby, God protected him from Pharaoh, who wanted to hurt him. He was rescued by Pharaoh's daughter, who took care of him as if he were her own baby. When Moses grew up and found out he was really a Hebrew, God told him to rescue his people and take them out of Egypt.**

Let's stand to tell the story of the amazing way God helped Moses take the Hebrews out of Egypt. Have kids stand. Instruct them to repeat after you, and have their puppets follow the motions.

Hi, my name is Moses. Hold Moses up and toward the children.

God saved me when I was a baby. Rock Moses in your arms.

He had a *big* job for me to do when I grew up. Move arms up and out in a big circle to show "big."

God wanted me to take all of his people out of Egypt. Point thumb to self, and walk your puppet in front of you.

But Pharaoh was a me-e-ean man! Put hands on hips and look mad.

I was afraid. Shake Moses to show he is trembling, then hide him behind your back.

But God told me he'd help me. Nod head, and bring Moses to the front.

So I went to see mean old Pharaoh. Walk in place, one hand on hip, with the puppet in front of you.

I said, "Let my people go!" Stop and hold Moses up and out.

Pharaoh wouldn't listen. Cover your ears.

Then things started to get interesting! Nod head.

God did some amazing things. Wave your hands over your head.

Finally, Pharaoh got smart. Tip puppet to your head and out.

He said, "Go and take your people with you!" Point Moses out in front of you, and walk in place.

I told all the people to follow me. Keep walking in place, look behind you, and beckon to "come."

We got out of there as fast as we could. Run in place.

We kept going and going and going and going. Keep running in place.

Suddenly we stopped. Stand still.

Oh no, the Red Sea was in front of us! Use the puppet to make a sweeping gesture left to right.

Praise Point

God does amazing things.

And Pharaoh's army was chasing us! Turn around, and look behind you.

We were stuck! We were afraid! Hug yourself, cringe, and tremble.

Suddenly I knew what to do. Stand up straight and tall.

I said, "God will help us!" Hold Moses up and out.

I stretched my staff out over the water. Move the puppet arm up so the twig is up in the air.

I prayed to God. Pause for a moment of silence.

Suddenly the water started moving! Move arms in a flowing motion.

The water separated down the middle! Clasp hands together, unclasp them, then move them out to the sides.

We could see the bottom of the sea—dry ground! Put hand over your eyes, looking out.

We walked straight across the bottom of that sea! Walk in place, smiling.

But we had to hurry because Pharaoh was still chasing us! Run in place.

They were right behind us, crossing the sea! Continue to run in place, then look over your shoulder.

Do you know what happened next? Stop and bend over with your hands on your knees.

The sea fell down around Pharaoh and his army! Make a whooshing sound and move your hand from left to right.

We were free! Jump up and down triumphantly.

We danced and praised God. Twirl around in a circle.

Then we thanked God because he did such an amazing thing. Kneel and pretend to pray.

Praise & Play With It

Say: **Let's follow Moses out of Egypt. Follow my Moses, and do what I do. When I say "freeze," everybody stop and stand still. Then say, "God does amazing things!"** Practice "freezing" and saying the phrase a few times. Then move around the room in Follow-the-Leader style. After a few minutes, say, "Freeze!" and wait for children to say the phrase.

Then appoint children and their Moses puppets to be the leaders until they say "freeze."

Talk About It

Ask:

• **What amazing thing did God do for Moses and the Hebrews?**

• **Why was that so amazing?**

• **What are some amazing things God does for us?**

• **How can we thank God when we see the amazing things he does?**

Puppet Pointer

Help kids understand that while they might not see lake or ocean waters separate, God does other amazing things for us every day. Point out things such as the rising and setting of the sun, soft cool winds that blow in the summer, rain that waters the earth, our food to eat, pets to love, and families to play with.

Power Prayer

God, you are amazing! Thank you that you are our God and that you love us. Help us to see all the amazing things you do every day. We thank you for those things. We love you.

25

Down, Down, Down!

Joshua and the Battle of Jericho

JOSHUA 6

Power Words

"He alone knows what we should do; he understands" (Job 12:13b, The Living Bible).

Provisions

Before class:

• In the story area, place two chairs back to back and far enough apart to stretch a blanket out over them. The children will march around the blanket when they pretend to march around the walls of Jericho.

• Bring a Bible to class.

For each child, you will need:

- a wooden spoon
- safety scissors
- brown, black, tan, or gold yarn
- wiggly craft eyes
- glue
- permanent markers

Prepare It

Gather the children around the table. Explain to them that they will make a two-sided puppet to help tell the story of Joshua and a famous battle he fought.

Give each child a wooden spoon. Show children how to glue on craft eyes and draw a mouth and nose on one side of the spoon. Then have children cut small pieces of yarn and glue the yarn to the spoons for hair. Explain that the other side of the spoon will be a trumpet. Show kids how to draw three circles on the handle for trumpet valves or keys.

Proclaim It

Gather children in the story area near the blanket "wall" with their Joshua puppets. Open your Bible to the book of Joshua, and show it to the children.

Say: **Today's story is about Joshua, and it comes from the Bible. Let's use our puppets to find out how Joshua learned that God knows best.**

Hold your puppet up and say hello to Joshua. One day God told Joshua to go to a city called Jericho. He wanted his people to live there. But there was a problem. There were lots of big, strong people already in that city, and they didn't want God's people around.

Joshua didn't know what to do. The people of Jericho would fight the Israelites from behind their big wall. Joshua didn't know how he could win a battle against Jericho. But God knows best. So he told Joshua just what to do. Have all the children form a circle around the blanket wall.

God told Joshua and his people to march around the city six times— once each day—and to blow on their trumpets. Show me how you'd make your puppet march around the walls. Good job! Now turn your puppet over, and show me how you'd blow the trumpet. Great!

Let's march around our wall six times. Some of you will be Joshua, and

God knows best.

some of you will be trumpeters. Each time we go around, we'll trade jobs. Form two groups. For example, have the girls be Joshua and the boys be the trumpeters. The second time around, have them switch jobs. After you've gone around the wall six times, have everyone stop and be quiet.

On the seventh day, God told them to march around the city seven times in one day and then give a mighty shout. Let's go around our wall one more time to show that Joshua marched seven times that day. Then we'll stop and give a mighty shout. Ready? Lead children around the wall one more time, stop, and then have everyone give a big shout.

Something amazing happened. Pull the blanket off the chairs. The walls came tumbling down! Joshua and his people won the city! And it was because God knew best and his people obeyed him.

Say: **Now let's be the walls of Jericho. We'll listen to Joshua give a shout. Then we'll come tumbling down.**

Have children stand in a circle. Appoint someone and his or her puppet to be "Joshua" and stand in the center of the circle. Say the following rhyme together while moving in a circle around Joshua. When Joshua calls out, "God knows best!" everyone should fall down and stop the rhyme, ending the game. Repeat, giving as many children a chance to be Joshua as time allows.

Round and round the walls we go
As many times as God says so.
Trumpet, trumpet play your tune.
Now give a shout that fills the room.

Power Prayer

God, you know best about everything! We praise you for that. We thank you that you love us and you help us when we need it, just as you helped Joshua. We love you, God, because you are so good.

Ask:

- **How did God help Joshua and his people?**
- **Why does God know best?**
- **Do you think God knows best about you? Tell us why you think that.**
- **How can we praise God for knowing what is best?**

Long and Strong

Samson

JUDGES 13; 16

Power Words

"If anyone loves me, he will obey my teaching" (John 14:23).

Provisions

Before class:

• Cut twenty-four-inch lengths of black or brown yarn for hair.

• Cut brown or black chenille wire into two-inch pieces.

• Bring a Bible to class.

For each child, you will need:

- an orange
- several whole cloves
- a cinnamon stick or craft stick
- a permanent marker
- safety scissors
- ten to twelve pieces of yarn
- chenille wire
- a napkin

Prepare It

Set out bowls of oranges, whole cloves, and cinnamon sticks, as well as several permanent markers. Set scissors in the story area. Gather the children around the table. Explain to them that they will make special puppets to help tell the story of someone who chose not to obey God's rules.

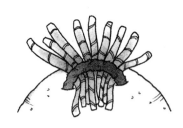

Give each child an orange, and show children how to stick cloves into it for eyes and a nose. Show them how to draw eyebrows over the clove eyeballs. Have them draw a mouth.

Have each child choose ten to twelve pieces of yarn and a piece of chenille wire. Show children how to bend the chenille wire into a small U shape. Lay the yarn across the top of the orange, and secure it in place by poking the ends of the U-shaped wire into the orange, straddling the yarn pieces. You may have to do this step for younger preschoolers.

Last of all, help children gently push a cinnamon stick or craft stick into the bottom of the orange for a handle. Use a napkin to wipe up the juice drips from the orange.

Encourage children to smell their puppets. Point out that when we love God and obey him, it's like a sweet smell to him and makes him happy in the same way our puppets have a sweet smell to us.

Proclaim It

Gather children in the story area with their Samson puppets. Open your Bible to Judges 13, and show it to the children.

Say: **Our Bible story comes from the book of Judges. It's about a man with long hair. Let's find out why Samson had long hair.**

Samson's mother wanted a baby very much. Finally, God answered her prayer, and she had a baby boy! **Cradle your Samson puppet in your arms like a baby.**

She named the baby Samson. To show he was special to God, Samson's mother promised never to cut his hair. **Hold up your Samson puppet and comb his long hair gently with your fingers.**

As Samson grew up, he obeyed this rule and never cut his hair. God blessed Samson and made him the strongest man ever. **Pump your arms up and down in the air to show how strong Samson was.** He was able to fight God's enemies all by himself. One time he even defeated a lion with his bare hands. **Walk your puppet on the floor in front of you. Now pretend he's fighting a big lion. Now hold him in the air to show he's the winner!** Thank you, God, for making Samson strong!

But Samson was only strong as long as he obeyed God and didn't cut his hair. **Now show me how strong you are by showing me your strong muscles—WOW! That's strong, and some of you don't even have long hair!**

One day Samson met a woman named Delilah. She tried to trick Samson and find out the secret of his strength. Delilah planned on telling the secret to Samson's enemies. They would pay her lots of money. So she begged and begged Samson to tell her. **Show me how Delilah begged by saying, "Please, please, please!"**

But Samson wouldn't tell his secret. **Turn your puppet left and right to show Samson saying no.** As long as Samson obeyed God's rule and didn't cut his hair, he stayed strong. But Delilah begged him so much that he finally gave in and told her the secret to his strength.

That night as Samson lay sleeping, Delilah had his hair cut off! **Use a pair of scissors to cut off the hair of your puppet.** Hand safety scissors to the children, and help them cut their puppets' hair.

What do you think happened? Sure enough, when Samson woke up, he was so weak that his enemies easily captured him. They threw him in prison. **Bend your knees and put your Samson puppet under them to show he's in prison.** Samson was sad that he had trusted Delilah. And he was very, very sad that he had disobeyed God.

After a long time, Samson's hair grew back, and he became strong again. He used his strength one last time to push down the building where his enemies were. Samson learned the hard way that it's important to obey God's rules.

Praise & Play With It

Ask:

- **What was God's rule for Samson?**
- **Did Samson obey God's rule?**
- **What are some rules God wants us to obey?**

Say: **God used Samson for good things when Samson obeyed. But when he disobeyed, he lost his strength and he couldn't do anything. Let's not be like Samson—let's obey God. His rules are meant to keep us safe and happy. Let's use our puppets to tell God that we think his rules are important.**

Have children spread out around the perimeter of the room, holding their puppets. Stand in the center and make statements one at a time, similar to the following:

- **We should obey our parents.**
- **We should hit one another.**
- **We should take toys away from each other.**
- **We should love God more than anything.**
- **We should help each other.**
- **We should share our toys.**
- **We should tell lies.**

Have children decide if it's a good rule to obey or not. If it is, they should nod their puppets to say yes, then take a step toward you in the center of the room saying, "It's important to obey God's rules." If it's not a good rule, they should stay where they are. When everyone reaches the center, jump up and down together and say, "Thank you, God, for loving us."

Have children smell their puppets again. Tell them whenever they smell their puppets to remember that when we obey God, to him it's like a sweet, happy smell. Encourage them to tell their families the story of Samson.

Power Prayer

God, help us to love you more than anything. Help us to obey your rules. We want to be strong to serve you every day. Thank you, God. We love you.

Talk About It

Ask:

- **What was God's rule for Samson?**
- **If Samson obeyed God, what would happen?**
- **How did Samson disobey God?**
- **Why is it important to obey God?**

Here I Am, Lord!

Samuel

I SAMUEL 1; 3

⭐ Power Words

"His God instructs him and teaches him the right way" (Isaiah 28:26).

⭐ Provisions

• Bring a Bible to class.

For each child, you will need:

• a washcloth or piece of fabric

• a rubber band

• a marker

• scissors

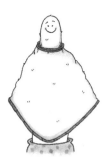

Prepare It

Gather the children around the table. Explain to them that they will make special puppets to help tell the story of a boy named Samuel who listened to God.

While children are watching, cover your index finger with a washcloth and form Samuel's head by winding a rubber band loosely around your finger at the first joint. Be sure not to wind it too tightly, or the rubber band will inhibit circulation and become uncomfortable.

Draw a smiley face on your covered fingertip to make Samuel's face. Wiggle your puppet at the children so they can see how their index fingers will help to form and move their puppets. Then give each child a washcloth, and help them make puppets of their own. When the rubber bands are in place, have an adult helper snip two small holes in each washcloth to create armholes for the puppet. Show children how to poke a thumb and little finger through the holes for Samuel's arms.

Puppet Pointer If you have very young preschoolers who have trouble keeping their index fingers inside the rubber band, give them unsharpened pencils to use instead.

Proclaim It

Gather the children in the story area with their Samuel puppets. Open your Bible to 1 Samuel 1, and show it to the children.

Say: **Today's story comes from the Bible. It's about a little boy named Samuel. You can help me tell Samuel's story today with your puppet. Drop your hand down to your side until the cloth hides Samuel's head. This is to show that Samuel isn't born yet. Let's begin our story there.**

Hannah wanted a baby. She prayed and prayed until God answered her. God gave her a beautiful baby boy! Lift up your hand now and show me baby Samuel. Have kids hold up their puppets.

Hannah loved Samuel and took good care of him. Have each child fold the corners of the washcloth up around baby Samuel to wrap him in a blanket. Then have each child hold Samuel in the other arm, rock him, and pretend to feed him.

Hannah said, "I give him to you, Lord, to serve you all of his life." Samuel grew and grew and became a little boy. Have each child drop the washcloth corners and hold the puppet up, sticking fingers out of Samuel's robe for arms. **One day while Samuel was still a little boy, his mother took him to live in the Temple. At the Temple, a man named Eli took care of Samuel and taught him to serve God.**

One night Samuel was sleeping. Lay hands on the floor to make "Samuel" sleep. **The Lord called Samuel.** Make Samuel stand up. **He ran to Eli and said, "Here I am." Can you say that?** Make Samuel run in place and say, "Here I am." **Eli said, "I did not call you; go back to bed." So Samuel went back to bed.** Make Samuel go back to bed. **Again the Lord called, "Samuel!"** Wake Samuel up. **Again Samuel got up and went to Eli—What do you think Samuel said?** Have kids say, "Here I am." **Eli said, "I did not call you, go back to bed." So Samuel did.** Make Samuel go back to bed again. **A third time God called, "Samuel!" Samuel ran to Eli—What do you think Samuel said?** Have puppets run and say, "Here I am!"

Then Eli realized that it was the Lord who was calling Samuel. He said, "Samuel, go and lie down. If God calls again, say, "Speak, Lord, I'm listening." So Samuel went to bed. Make Samuel sleep. **Sure enough, God called him. "Samuel! Samuel!" What did Samuel say?** Give children time to answer. **Yes, Samuel said, "Speak, Lord, I'm listening."**

Then God told Samuel some important things. Samuel did everything God told him to do. From that day forward, God spoke to Samuel often. Even when he was a grown-up, Samuel told the people to love and obey God. He told them to quit being bad. Samuel listened to and obeyed God all his life. Samuel loved God, and God loved Samuel.

★ Praise & Play With It 🎵

Say: **God spoke to Samuel, and Samuel listened. God speaks to us, too. We probably won't hear God call our name out loud like Samuel did, but he does talk to us.**

God talks to us through the Bible. God gave us the Bible to tell us about himself.

God talks to us by the things he made. He uses the big sky, the sun, the moon, the stars, the pretty flowers and trees, and all his special animals to say, "I love you and I made these for you!"

God talks to us through our parents and teachers when they say things like "I love you" or "Jesus loves you."

Let's play a game to thank God that he speaks to us. Find a spot in the room for you and your puppet to lie down and pretend to sleep, like the way Samuel did in the Temple. Wait while children find a place to lie down.

**When I call your name, put your puppet in the air and say, "Here I am."
Then listen while I tell you something God says to you. Then say, "Thank
you, God."**

Call each child by name. Make the following statements or make up your
own. Give each child time to answer, "Thank you, God."

- **Jesus loves you.**
- **God says you're important.**
- **Jesus knows all about you and likes you.**
- **Jesus wants you for a friend.**
- **God says you're special.**

Talk About It

Ask:

- **How did God talk to Samuel?**
- **What did Samuel do when God called him?**
- **How does God talk to you?**
- **What should you do when you hear God talk to you?**

Power Prayer

*God, thank you that you
speak to us! Help us to be
like Samuel. We want to
love you, listen to you,
and obey you. We love
you, Lord.*

Mighty Little

David and Goliath

1 SAMUEL 17

"The battle is the Lord's" (1 Samuel 17:47b).

Before class:

• Cut butcher paper into 22x48-inch pieces. Fold the pieces in half, creating 22x24-inch pieces. Tape the sides together from the bottom open end up about ten inches to form a bag or pouch.

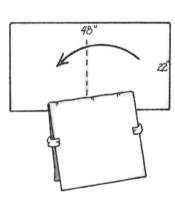

• On a piece of poster board or butcher paper draw Goliath's mean face, and tape it to a wall away from the story area, with the bottom edge about six feet off the floor.

• Set five beanbags or wads of paper on the floor under the poster drawing.

• Bring a Bible to class.

37

For each child, you will need:

- a folded and taped piece of butcher paper
- tape
- safety scissors
- a pencil
- markers

Prepare It

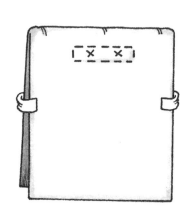

Gather the children around the table. Explain to them that they will make special puppets to help tell the story of David who fought a giant when he was just a boy.

Give each child one of the folded pieces of butcher paper. Explain that they will make puppets that are big enough for them to fit inside. Slip a folded piece of paper over each child's head, and have him or her stick arms out of the openings above the tape. If the tape is up too high, cut it with scissors. If the tape's not high enough, add more. With your fingers, carefully locate where the child's eyes are behind the paper. Carefully mark the spot with a pencil. Then remove the paper from his or her head. Cut a narrow rectangular window for the child to look through, approximately 2x4 inches. Ask children to decorate their bag puppets to look like David by adding hair and facial features.

Proclaim It

Help children put on their David puppets, and gather in the story area. Open your Bible to the book of 1 Samuel, and show it to the children.

Say: **Today we have big puppets to tell the story of a little boy who did a big thing. When you hear me say the word "little," hold your hands a little bit apart and bend over a little bit to make yourself smaller.** Show children the action. **When you hear me say the word "big," spread your hands far apart and stand up straight and big.** Show children the action.

David was a <u>little</u> shepherd boy. What do shepherds do? That's right, they take care of the sheep—<u>big</u> ones and <u>little</u> ones. Show me how you'd take care of sheep. Good job!

One day David's father sent him on a journey. It wasn't a <u>little</u> journey, it was a <u>big</u> journey. He wanted David to check on his brothers who were fighting a <u>big</u> battle far away. He wanted David to take them some food and

to see how they were doing. **Pack up bread and cheese as David did. Now let's go!** Walk to a spot near the wall with the Goliath poster. For safety's sake, make sure there is no furniture on the path from the story area to the wall.

When David got to the battle he saw a <u>big</u>, mean person. Put your hand above your eyes, and look up at the poster on the wall. **That's Goliath. He's a giant. He made everyone feel <u>little</u>. He hated the Israelites. He hated David. And he hated God.**

All the people were afraid of him, even David's brothers. But when Goliath said bad things about God, David got mad. Why did no one stop this bully, he wondered? Why did everyone run away? Well, David wasn't going to run away. No! He might be <u>little</u>, but he would fight and he would win because his God was <u>big</u>!

Everybody said he couldn't do it. The people said he was too <u>little</u>. But David knew that God was stronger than anything! And God was bigger than Goliath!

So David picked up five smooth, <u>little</u> stones. Let's pretend to pick up five stones. Let's count—one, two, three, four, five. That's enough! David went up to Goliath and shouted, "The battle is the Lord's!" Shout that with me. Shout it <u>little</u>. Shout it <u>big</u>!

Whisper the next part to get their attention. **Then David did something that surprised everyone. He threw one of his <u>little</u> stones at Goliath.** Hit your forehead. **SMACK! That <u>little</u> stone hit <u>big</u> Goliath right between the eyes! It hit him so hard that he fell right over. Let's give a <u>big</u> clap for God!**

Everyone was happy and joyful. The people danced and sang and celebrated. They all learned an important lesson that day: No matter how <u>little</u> you are, God is <u>bigger</u> than any bad thing in life, even a giant like Goliath!

Praise & Play With It

Say: **David was afraid, but he was brave. He knew that God was on his side. He knew that God was bigger and better and mightier than any person could ever be, even if that person was a mean old giant.**

Tell children to think of things that scare them.

Say: **God is bigger and stronger than any of the things that scare us. Let's pretend that the poster is not Goliath, but the thing that we're afraid of. We're going to throw stones like David did and say, "The battle is the Lord's!" God can help us get rid of our fears.**

Have the children take turns standing in front of the Goliath poster, naming out loud the one thing they're afraid of, such as big dogs, the dark, or Mom and Dad leaving them with babysitters. Then have the child say, "The battle is the Lord's!" Have him or her throw beanbags at the Goliath poster until it is hit. Lower the poster or move it higher as needed to challenge your group. Remind the children that God is bigger than their fears and that he'll help them overcome the things that scare them.

Talk About It

Ask:

- **What big thing did David do?**
- **Why was that so amazing?**
- **Who helped David? In what ways?**
- **How does God help you?**

Power Prayer

God, thank you for helping David, even though he was little. Thank you that the battle is yours. Help us to be brave when we need to be. Help us do big things for you. We love you, God.

Beauty and the Beast

Esther

ESTHER 1–10

"I can do everything through him who gives me strength" (Philippians 4:13).

Provisions

Before class:

• Hot glue four or five chenille wires to the head of each sock puppet for hair.

• Set up a hand-washing station at the table by filling a basin with warm water and setting some fragrant soap and hand towels next to it.

• Prepare a tray of fruit pieces such as bananas and oranges.

• Bring scissors and a Bible to class.

Puppet Pointer To keep bananas from turning brown, cut them into sections but don't remove the peels.

For each child, you will need:

- a child-sized white sock
- four or five brown, yellow, or black chenille wires
- stick-on jewels
- old perfume, cologne, or body spray
- hand lotion
- markers
- safety scissors
- blush (optional)
- gold star garland or aluminum foil
- a few pieces of fruit
- a napkin

Prepare It

Explain to the children that they will make special puppets to tell the story of a brave girl named Esther.

Say: **Today's Bible story is about a brave girl named Esther.** Show children the book of Esther in the Bible. **I'm going to tell you part of our story as we prepare our puppets.**

One time the king of the land was looking for a new queen. He brought all the pretty young women in his kingdom to his palace. He told his servants to get them ready with sweet-smelling things, new clothes, and jewels. Then he would choose one of them to be his new queen.

One of the girls at the palace was named Esther. She was beautiful on the inside and on the outside. She loved God and didn't want to be the queen, but she obeyed the king's command anyway.

Let's do some of the things Esther did to get ready. Have the kids wash and dry their hands. Encourage them to smell the soap, and feel the warmth of the water and the softness of the towels. Then give them each a dab of hand lotion, and encourage them to feel the cool sleekness of the lotion and smell its fragrance as they rub it in. Tell them to feel how soft their hands are after the lotion is gone. Explain that Esther and the other women took long baths with soaps, perfumes, and lotions. Set the basin of water and towels aside.

Say: **After the women took their baths, they were given new clothing and jewelry to get them ready to see the king. Let's get our Esther puppets ready to see the king.**

Give children the prepared socks, and have them slip their hands inside. Have an adult helper snip two holes in each sock puppet so children can put their fingers through the holes for puppet arms. Give kids blue, brown, or green markers to draw eyes on their puppets, and pink markers to draw mouths. Allow them to smudge some pink blush on their puppets for pink cheeks or to use a pink marker. Show them how to wind the chenille wire around their fingers to make curly hair. Give each child some stick-on jewels or stickers to attach for clothing decorations and jewelry. Have each child make a crown with the gold star garland or aluminum foil. Set the crowns aside. Last of all, have them dab a little perfume onto their puppets.

As children work, talk with them about all the good things God made for us to enjoy—things that smell good, feel good, look good, and taste good. When the puppets are finished, clear away the craft supplies. Bring out the tray of fruit.

Say: **While Esther was at the palace, the people ate good food so they would stay healthy and strong.** Allow children to choose a few pieces of fruit and a napkin. Before they eat, have them describe how the different fruit looks, then how it smells, feels, and tastes. If children want to, they can pretend to feed their Esther puppets.

Proclaim It

Set a folded piece of paper and the crowns in the story area. Have children stand away from the story area with their puppets on their hands.

Say: **After several weeks of preparation, the king was finally ready to choose his new queen.** Go sit on a chair in the story area and pretend to be the king. Have the children walk up to you one at a time, and show you their puppets. Then have the children sit down. When everyone is seated, continue: **You all look great! You smell good, too! When the king saw Esther, he loved her. She was the one he wanted to be the queen.** Give each child a crown to put on his or her puppet's head.

Esther was a good queen because she loved God. One day she found out that the king's bad servant had made a law to get rid of all of her people, the

Puppet Pointer Most preschool boys will freely participate in this activity. But if a boy doesn't want to make an Esther puppet, his puppet can be the king. Simply cut the hair shorter and omit the pink cheeks. Tell children that men like to be clean and smell good too. King puppets could act out the king's part in the "Proclaim It" activity.

Puppet Pointer You can also give each child a small piece of fabric for a cape, and tie it to the puppet with a pretty ribbon.

Jews. Her uncle sent her a message. Unfold the piece of paper, and pretend to read it. **It said, "Esther, you must go to the king and explain that the Jews are your people. You must change his mind. Tell him not to do it. You must save your people."**

Esther wanted to save her people. But the king had a very strict rule: You had to be invited to see him. Although Esther was not invited, she needed to talk to the king to save her people. This made Esther very afraid. Show me how Esther looked when she was afraid.

Before going to see the king, Esther and her people prayed to God for help. Let's get on our knees and pretend to pray. Then Esther said, "I will go to the king to help my people."

Make your puppet say, "I must help my people." Say, "God will help me." Esther was very brave. She went to the king even though she wasn't asked. But the king wasn't angry with Esther! Instead, he loved her. He said, "Esther, what do you want? How can I help you?" Esther told him about the plan to hurt her people. The king was angry. Show me an angry face.

But the king wasn't angry with Esther! He was angry with the bad servant. The king saved the Jews from being hurt, and he got rid of the bad servant. Esther was beautiful on the inside and on the outside. God helped her to be a good and brave queen, who helped her people.

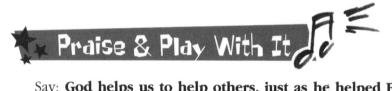

Say: **God helps us to help others, just as he helped Esther. We can be brave too, and we can help people the way that she did.**

Have the kids name brave things they can do and ways they can help others.

Then have children choose a partner. Tell them to use their puppets to act out a situation where they help someone or do something brave. Then have kids take turns acting out the situation for the rest of the class. Be prepared to give children suggestions if they need them.

When everyone has had a chance to show helping or brave actions, say together, "Thank you, God, for helping us to help others."

Talk About It

Ask:

- **What did Esther do that was brave?**
- **In what way did God help Esther?**
- **What brave things have you done?**
- **In what ways can you help others?**

Power Prayer

Lord, thank you that you helped Esther save her people. We want to be brave and help others too. We thank you and praise you for helping us. We love you, Lord.

The Boy King

Josiah

2 CHRONICLES 34–35

"Taste and see that the Lord is good" (Psalm 34:8).

Before class:

• Cut purple or blue felt into a 4x5-inch rectangle to make a cape for each child's puppet. The cape should be wide enough to go halfway around the open edge of a cup.

• Put the powder from an instant pudding mix into a resealable bag. You'll need enough powder to make a serving of pudding for each child.

• Put the correct amount of milk for the pudding powder into a sealed container. If a refrigerator is not available at class, put the milk in a small cooler with ice. You'll also need a bowl and a mixing spoon.

• Cut the instructions off the pudding box, and put them, along with the resealable bag of pudding powder, inside an empty box. Gift-wrap the box to look like a "treasure" box.

• Bring a Bible to class.

• Set up a CD player with a CD of lively children's worship songs.

For each child, you will need:
• a white plastic foam cup

• two wiggly craft eyes

• glue

• a foil baking cup

• adhesive jewels or stickers

• markers

• a piece of felt

• colored electrical tape

• a plastic spoon and a napkin

• a small paper cup

• pudding

• M&M's mini chocolate candies

Prepare It

Gather the children around the table. Have each child put a hand inside an inverted plastic foam cup. Explain that kids will turn their cups into puppets that will help tell the story about a boy named Josiah. Tell them that Josiah was a boy who became king when he was only eight years old.

Help each child tape a felt cape piece to the narrow bottom edge of the cup with colored electrical tape so the cape hangs down the arm when the puppet is put on. Make the tape go around the entire circumference of the cup edge to form a collar.

Next have each child glue two wiggly craft eyes on the face and a foil baking cup to the puppet's head for a crown. Have the children draw facial features with the markers. Last of all, give each child several stick-on jewels or stickers to decorate the crown, collar, and cape of the puppet.

Set the milk near the table. Put the bowl, mixing spoon, plastic spoons, small paper cups, M&M's, and napkins on the table.

Gather children in the story area with their Josiah puppets. Open your Bible to 2 Chronicles 34, and show it to the children.

Say: **When Josiah was only eight years old, his father died. Say, "Poor Josiah!" But God had special plans for Josiah. Josiah became the king! Do you know someone who is eight years old? Imagine him or her being a king or queen! That's how it was for Josiah.**

Praise Point

God's Word is good.

When Josiah was sixteen years old, the Bible says that he began to seek God. That means he prayed and wanted to know all about God. You know how you feel when you're hungry for food—well, that's how Josiah felt about God. He wanted to know God. He looked for God the way someone would look for a great treasure. Let's take our Josiah puppets on a treasure hunt, and see if we can find some treasure. Have children make their puppets look around the room until they discover the treasure box you made.

A few years later, Josiah wanted to show his respect for God, so he started to clean up the Temple where people used to worship. No one had taken care of the Temple for a long time, and it was all broken down and in bad shape. While they were cleaning it up, they found a treasure and brought it to Josiah. It was the Book of the Law of the Lord! It had been lost a long time. Let's look in our treasure box.

Open the box and take out the pudding mix and instructions.

Hmm...I wonder what kind of treasure this is? Open the resealable bag and smell it, then pretend to read the directions.

This says that if we add milk to the powder it will become a delicious snack. I think this is pudding! Let's follow these directions and see. Move the group over to the table.

Josiah was so excited that they found the Book of the Lord. He read it, and studied it, and talked to God about it. He loved God's Word! Then he taught it to his people and made sure they obeyed God. Let's follow our directions in the same way that Josiah followed God's directions. Let's make something good!

Let the children take turns pouring the powder in the bowl, adding the milk, and stirring. Then put the bowl in the refrigerator to chill while you continue with the "Praise and Play With It" activity.

Praise & Play With It

Say: **While the pudding chills, let's use our puppets to praise God because his Word is good.** Turn on some lively children's worship songs and have the children dance with their puppets to praise God. When you stop the music, have the children "freeze." Then have a few children take turns saying, "God's Word is good."

Praise and play for several minutes, then gather around the table again. Have children spoon the pudding into individual paper cups and distribute napkins and spoons.

Say: **There's a verse in the Bible that says, "Taste and see that the Lord is good." When Josiah found God's Word, it was like finding a great, tasty treasure to him. Before we eat our pudding, let's thank God that his Word is good.**

Give each child a small handful of M&M's. Before eating the pudding, have children each add a mini chocolate candy to their cups every time someone finishes the sentence, "God is good because…"

Talk About It

Ask:

- **Was Josiah a good king or bad king? Why?**
- **When Josiah found God's Word, what did he do with it?**
- **How can you obey God's Word?**
- **How can you show God that you love him and his Word?**

Power Prayer

Dear God, thank you for helping Josiah find your Word. We want to love your Word and obey you just as Josiah did. Help us to tell others about your Word, too, just as Josiah did. We love you, Lord!

Turn Up the Heat!

The Fiery Furnace

DANIEL 3

"He is our help and our shield" (Psalm 33:20b).

Before class:

• Construct a "fiery furnace" from an empty cardboard box by cutting off the top flaps. Cut a window in the front of the box. Cover the window with red cellophane, and tape it to the inside of the box. On one end of the box, cut a hole just large enough to put a flashlight into.

• Tear off four- to five-inch pieces of aluminum foil. You'll need two pieces for each child, plus a few extras for experimenting.

• Bring a flashlight and a Bible to class.

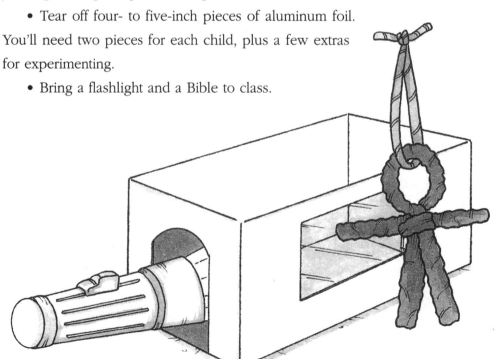

For each child, you will need:
- aluminum foil
- a piece of yarn or string

Prepare It

Gather the children around the table. Explain to them that they will make special puppets to tell the story of Shadrach, Meshach, and Abednego.

Give each child a piece of aluminum foil. Show them how to roll or crumple the foil along the long edge to shape it into a foil stick. Bend the "stick" at the center, making a loop for a head, and twist it twice at the neck. The ends hanging down are the legs. Give each child a second piece of foil, and have him or her crumple it the same way as the first. Wrap this piece twice around the neck of the foil figure to make the arms. Fold the ends of the arms so they're the right length.

Then give each child a length of yarn or string, and help him or her tie it to the loop head. Show children how to dangle the figures like marionettes. Be sure to make a puppet for yourself for the "Proclaim It" activity. Make it slightly larger than the others.

Proclaim It

Set the fiery furnace and a flashlight on a low chair or stool in the story area.

Gather children in the story area with their foil puppets. Open your Bible to Daniel 3, and show it to the children.

Say: **Our Bible story comes from the book of Daniel. It's about three men who loved God very much. Dangle your puppet, and make it dance on the floor to show that the three men loved God and were happy to worship him.**

The men's names were Shadrach, Meshach, and Abednego. Those are funny names! Let's practice saying them together. Have kids say the names a few times. **Shadrach, Meshach, and Abednego worked in a place called Babylon. The king there built a great big golden statue. He said that all the people must bow down to it and worship it. If they did not worship it, they would immediately be thrown into a fiery furnace. But Shadrach, Meshach, and Abednego would not worship the statue. Why do you think they wouldn't worship the statue?**

They would only worship God. The king was angry with them and ordered

them to be thrown into the fiery furnace. Put the furnace in the center of the story area. Wiggle the flashlight inside the flap to make it look like a fire.

Shadrach, Meshach, and Abednego said, "O king, our God can save us from the fire. But even if he does not, we will not serve your gods or worship your golden statue."

Praise Point

God protects us.

This made the king furious! He was so mad that he made the fire seven times hotter than before! Then he ordered his strongest servants to throw Shadrach, Meshach, and Abednego into the furnace. The fire was so hot that the servants were burned as they threw Shadrach, Meshach, and Abednego into the furnace. Let's put our figures into the fire. Have three children at a time dangle their figures in the furnace while you wiggle the flashlight. Give everyone a chance to put his or her figure in the fire. Ask three children to leave their figures in the furnace while you finish the story. Slip your puppet into the fire with theirs.

Suddenly the king leaped to his feet in amazement. "Didn't we throw three men in there?" he asked.

The people replied, "Yes, O king, three men."

"Look!" said the king, "I see four men walking around in the fire and none of them are hurt."

The king went to the furnace and yelled for Shadrach, Meshach, and Abednego to come out of the fire. Pull the puppets out of the furnace one at a time.

Everyone was amazed. The fire had not harmed the men, not a hair on their heads was burned, their robes weren't black, and there was no smell of fire on them!

The king said, "Praise the God of Shadrach, Meshach, and Abednego! He alone can save and protect this way. No other god can do this." After that, the king gave the three men good jobs and told all the people to honor God. God protected Shadrach, Meshach, and Abednego.

Praise & Play With It

Say: **We saw how God protected Shadrach, Meshach, and Abednego from the fire. God protects us, too. He gives us parents and teachers to take care of us and keep us safe. He watches over us and loves us. Let's use our puppets to praise God for protecting us.**

Sing the following rhyme to the tune of "Pop! Goes the Weasel." Have kids take turns by threes, dangling their puppets in the furnace while another child wiggles the flashlight.

The furnace was hot and burning with flames.

The three were tossed into it.

God protected all three of them.

Out! They came a dancing!

On the last phrase, have kids lift their puppets out of the furnace and dance them on the floor. Repeat the activity until everyone has a turn.

Talk About It

Ask:

- **How did God protect Shadrach, Meshach, and Abednego?**
- **Why did God protect them?**
- **How does God protect you?**
- **What are some ways we can praise God for protecting us?**

Power Prayer

Dear Jesus, we love the story of how you protected Shadrach, Meshach, and Abednego! Thank you for showing us how strong and mighty you are. Thank you for protecting us, too. We worship you and love you, God!

Lion Around

Daniel and the Lions

DANIEL 6

"The angel of the Lord encamps around those who fear him, and he delivers them" (Psalm 34:7).

Before class:

• Cut curly brown craft hair into small pieces.

• Cut two-inch high triangles out of both brown and gold construction paper and slightly smaller triangles out of black paper.

• Cut broom straws or chenille wire into three-inch lengths.

• Cut eyeholes from a paper plate for each child. Measure the plate on a preschooler to get the correct position before you cut.

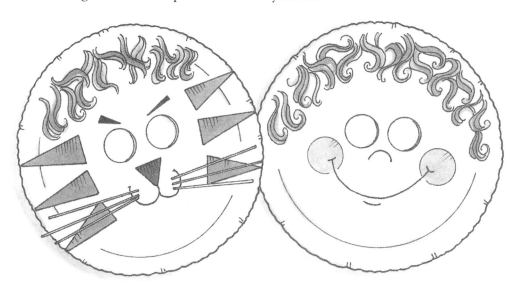

54

- Gather plastic berry containers or bowls for class.
- Bring a Bible to class.

For each child, you will need:
- a white paper plate with eyeholes
- curly craft hair
- construction paper triangles to fit around the edge of the paper plate
- six broom straws or chenille wires
- glue
- markers
- animal crackers

 Prepare It

Gather the children around the table. Explain to them that they will make special puppets to tell the story of Daniel and the night he slept with lions.

Give each child a paper plate with the eyeholes cut out. First, have children decorate one side of their plates as Daniel. Encourage them to draw facial features on him with the markers and then glue some curly craft hair at the top for his hair. Have them carefully flip their plates over and glue the brown and gold paper triangles along the edge of the plates—the triangle tips pointing out, but not hanging over the edge of the plates. Help them draw slanted triangles over the eyeholes to make the lions look fierce. (See illustration.)

Show them how to glue a black triangle in the center for a nose, draw a double U shape for a muzzle, and glue on six broom straws for whiskers.

Puppet Pointer Try using brown curly craft hair for both the lion's mane and Daniel's hair.

Give the puppet masks a little time to dry while children help you clean up the craft supplies. Then distribute handfuls of animal crackers, and instruct children to find all the lion cookies and put them into plastic berry containers or bowls. Set the containers aside to use later.

Proclaim It

Create a "lions' den" near the story area by putting chairs in a circle facing outward or by laying a blanket on the floor. Make the lions' den big enough for everyone to fit inside or on.

Gather children in the story area with their puppets. Open your Bible to Daniel 6, and show it to the children. As you tell the story, use your puppet, showing the Daniel side when speaking about Daniel and the lion side when speaking about the lions.

Say: **Today's story comes from the Bible. Hold the face side of your puppet up and look at me through it. Wave to me and say, "Hello, Daniel!"**

Daniel was a man who loved God with all his heart. One time the king made a law that everyone should worship and pray only to him, not to anyone else. Daniel wouldn't do that. Daniel would only pray to God. Shake your head "no" to show that Daniel wouldn't pray to the king.

The king's law said that if anyone prayed or worshipped any other God, he or she would be thrown into a den of hungry lions. Show me your lion puppet. Put it to your face, and growl at me the way a hungry lion would. Oh, scary!

Daniel was afraid. He would be safe if he obeyed the king and worshipped him. But then he'd break God's law, which said to obey only God. So Daniel did something very important. He prayed to God and asked for help. Let's show our Daniel face and kneel on the floor as Daniel did when he prayed.

One day the king discovered that Daniel was still praying to God and not worshipping the king. What do you think happened? Yes, he took Daniel and threw him into a pit with lions in it! Hold up your Daniel puppet. Come on, Daniel, into the lions' den you go! Have everyone go inside the circle of chairs.

The lions were roaring and hungry and fierce! Use your lion masks, and show me how fierce they were.

Praise Point

God keeps us safe.

Just when Daniel thought he was in big trouble, something amazing happened! God sent an angel to shut the lions' mouths so they couldn't bite Daniel! All they could do was look at Daniel! Show me how the lions looked.

God kept Daniel safe. In the morning, the king hurried to the lions' den. He called out, "Daniel, has your God rescued you from the lions?"

"Yes, O king! My God sent his angel, and he shut the mouths of the lions. They didn't hurt me."

The king was amazed. He lifted Daniel out of the den. Move the children back to the story area. **Not one scratch or wound or scrape was found on Daniel. He had trusted God to save him.**

The king believed in God because of what happened to Daniel. He made a new law that told everyone that Daniel's God was the living God. They were to respect and honor him.

Praise & Play With It

Say: **In our story today, we learned that Daniel obeyed God, and God kept Daniel safe. The lions obeyed God too, and they didn't hurt Daniel. Let's play a game to show that Daniel and the lions obeyed God. When I call out instructions to you, pretend to obey God and do what I say. When the instructions are for Daniel, use your Daniel puppet. If the instructions are for the lions, use your lion puppet.**

Call out instructions to "Daniel" and the "lions" alternately. Ask Daniel to do things such as pray, tell others about God, and help a neighbor with a chore. Give the lions instructions to lie down, purr, run, and curl in a ball. End by having the lions sit quietly in a circle on the floor or around the table. Bring out the bowl of lion crackers that were sorted earlier.

Say: **Daniel obeyed God because he loved him. God kept Daniel safe. God keeps us safe, too. Let's thank God for keeping us safe.** Have children tell ways that God keeps them safe. Remind them that God gave them parents, teachers, and friends to watch out for them and to keep them safe, just as he sent the angel to keep Daniel safe. Have each child say, "Thank you, God, for keeping me safe." Then have each one take a lion cookie as a snack.

Puppet Pointer

If there aren't enough lion cookies for everyone, offer other animal crackers, and have children pretend they're lions.

Talk About It

Ask:

- **Who did Daniel obey? Why?**
- **How did God keep Daniel safe?**
- **How does God keep us safe?**
- **What are some ways you can help keep others safe?**

Power Prayer

Lord, thank you that you keep us safe. You are stronger than a lion and more powerful than a whole den of lions! Watch over us and protect us. Help us to serve you the way Daniel did. We love you, God!

I Don't Want To!

Jonah

JONAH 1–4

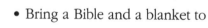 **Power Words**

"Obey me, and I will be your God" (Jeremiah 7:23b).

 Provisions

Before class:

• Cut large fish shapes about 6x12 inches out of different colored poster board.

• Photocopy the Jonah figure shown, trace it on poster board, then cut the figures out. You'll need one figure for each child. Adjust the size of the figure to fit comfortably inside the fish you cut.

• Bring a Bible and a blanket to class.

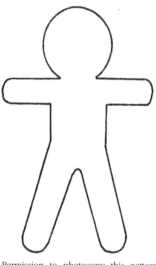

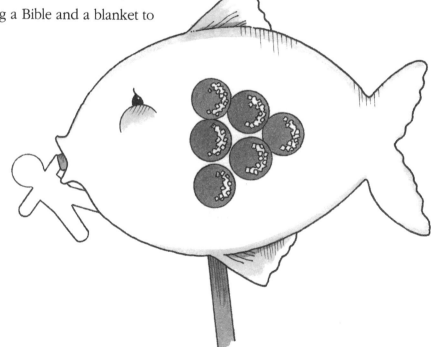

For each child, you will need:

- one fish shape
- one Jonah shape
- a clip-style clothespin
- tape
- colored dot stickers
- markers
- glitter glue
- a stick such as a wooden dowel, an unsharpened pencil, or a craft stick

Prepare It

Gather the children around the table. Explain to them that they will make special puppets to tell the story of the day Jonah was swallowed by a giant fish.

Have children choose a Jonah shape and a fish shape. Have them draw facial features and other details on them. Give children several dot stickers (or have them draw dots with markers) to decorate their fish. Show them how to make scales on the fish with glitter glue.

Help each child tape a clothespin to the back of the fish about an inch or so from the edge of the mouth. Then help each child tape a dowel on the back of the fish toward the bottom for a handle.

Puppet Pointer Since glitter glue takes a while to dry, you may want to have the children decorate their fish after the "Proclaim It" and "Praise and Play With It" activities.

Proclaim It

Gather children in the story area with their Jonah and fish puppets. Open your Bible to the book of Jonah, and show it to the children.

Say: **Let's use our puppets to tell the story of a man named Jonah. One day God told Jonah to go to a city called Nineveh. God said, "Jonah, go to Nineveh and tell the people to stop being bad and start being good."**

Do you know what Jonah said? What would you say if you were Jonah? Well, Jonah said, "No, God, I don't want to!"

Have you ever said no to your mom or dad when they told you to do something? Then you know how Jonah was feeling! And you know he was disobeying. Let's find out what happened to him.

As you read the following story to the children, make up motions for the figures to do. For example, in the beginning you might point to different children's fish that have the colors and shapes mentioned. Then "run" your Jonah puppet, and have him jump into your hand for a boat. Toss him "overboard" when you say, "There goes Jonah—over the side!"

When you get to the part about the fish swallowing Jonah, clip the clothespin on your puppet's head. At first leave Jonah's feet sticking out, then put him "in" all the way. When the fish spits Jonah out, pinch the clothespin to drop Jonah. Have children move their puppets, too.

Say:

One fish, two fish,
Three fish, and more.
Big fish, blue fish,
Huge fish galore!

This one has a dot.
This one has a spot.
My, oh my, what a lot
Of dots and spots!

Here comes Jonah.
He likes to run.
He likes to run,
But not for fun.

He won't listen.
He won't mind.
From God he runs.
He must be blind.

He runs fast and he runs far.
What does he do?
What does he say?
"I'll take this ship—
    it's going my way!

"It's great! It'll do.
Just get me away from you.
Near or far, far or near,
I just wanna get out of here!"

A storm comes up.
It rocks the boat.
Now it dips—
But will it float?

Oh me! Oh my!
Oh, what a ride!
There goes Jonah—
Over the side!

Down, down, down
Jonah goes.
Where he'll land,
Only God knows!

Oh my, oh me!
Look what's swimming
    past my knee!
It's one fish, two fish, maybe more.
Jonah has a surprise in store.

Gulp! Goes a great big fish,
What a yummy dish!
"Help!" screams Jonah too late,
"He made me his dinner date!"

Down in the belly
Of that great big fish,
Jonah was sloshing,
Jonah went squish.

But Jonah got smart
And he softened his heart.
"I'm sorry, Lord, I'll obey!
Just rescue me, I pray.

"Oh, do not delay!
Oh, do not take long!
I'll do what you say,
Even sing you a song.

"I'll go here, I'll go there.
Yes, Lord, I'll go anywhere!"

Then what did that big fish do?
Ka-burp! And ka-bump!
Ka-flish! And ka-flump!
Out he spit Jonah in one messy
    lump!

Up went Jonah,
And away he ran.
All the way to Nineveh
To accomplish God's plan!

Praise & Play With It

Have kids set their fish puppets aside. Have them hold their Jonah figures, and stand together in a group.

Say: **God wants us to obey him. Let's play a game to help us remember how Jonah learned to obey God. When I say, "God says go to Nineveh, Jonah!" hold up your Jonah figure and say, "No, no, I won't go!" Then I'm going to send a great big fish to swallow you up!** Shake and wiggle the blanket to show them that it's the fish. **After I cover you with the blanket, you say, "Yes, yes, I'll obey!" Then I'll tell you where to find "Nineveh."**

Play the game several times. Each time choose a different spot in the room to be Nineveh. Then have that spot be the beginning for the new game. Children love repetition and soon will be able to tell the story of Jonah just from playing the game!

Talk About It

Ask:

• **What did God tell Jonah to do?**

• **Did Jonah obey God? Explain.**

• **Why did Jonah change his mind?**

• **Why is it important for us to obey?**

• **How does God help us obey?**

Just Say Yes!

An Angel Appears to Mary

LUKE 1:26-56

Power Words

"The Lord is faithful to all his promises" (Psalm 145:13b).

Provisions

Before class:

• Cut eleven-inch squares from pieces of white, lacy, gold, or silver fabric.

• For angel wings, fold six-inch paper doilies in half, and glue the insides together with several dots of glue. Make sure these are dry before class. Make a few extras to have on hand in the event of rips or tears.

• If not already in small pieces, cut craft hair into about six-inch lengths.

• Gently poke a ¾-inch deep hole in each plastic foam ball with a sharpened pencil.

- Be sure a low-heat glue gun or stapler will be on hand.
- Bring a Bible to class.

For each child, you will need:
- an unsharpened pencil
- an eleven-inch square of fabric
- one plastic foam ball (about two inches in diameter, but not larger)
- markers
- a few lengths of gold curly craft hair
- one self-adhesive Velcro circle
- a doily glued in half

 **Puppet Pointer** If you use craft items instead of unsharpened pencils (such as wooden dowels), make sure you adjust the size of the fabric, balls, and doilies to the right proportions.

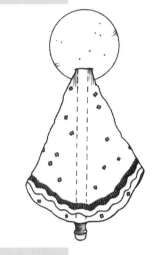

Prepare It

Gather the children around the table. Explain to them that they will make special puppets to tell the story of the day Mary was visited by an angel.

Have each child choose a plastic foam ball, an unsharpened pencil, and a piece of fabric. Show them how to put the end of the pencil in the center of the fabric and insert it into the hole in the ball. Then show them how to draw a face on the ball with markers.

Have children select a few lengths of craft hair. Ask an adult helper to use a low-heat glue gun or stapler to attach the hair to the head (be sure this step is done out of children's reach). To attach the wings, help each child stick one part of a Velcro circle on the fabric at the back of the angel and the other part on the center of the doily "wings." Have children practice gently putting on and taking off the wings once or twice. Explain that their puppets are "Mary," and then, when the wings are added, they become the "angel." Collect the angel wings from the children, and take them with you to the story area.

Puppet Pointer Permanent, fine-tipped Sharpie markers work the best and leave the darkest color on plastic foam. However, if you decide to use permanent markers, supervise the children closely so they don't mark themselves or their clothing.

Proclaim It

Gather children in the story area with their Mary puppets. Open your Bible to Luke 1, and show it to the children.

Say: **Our story today comes from the book of Luke in the Bible. Mary was a girl who grew up loving God with all her heart.** Point your Mary puppet in the air toward heaven to show that Mary loved God.

Mary prayed. Fold your hands, and keep your puppet between them. **Mary told God she would do anything he wanted. She would obey him and be his servant. Besides praying, Mary served God by her many little daily jobs.** Have children briefly act out the following with their puppets after you say each one. Say:

- **She cooked food for her family.**
- **She cleaned the house.**
- **She was kind to everyone.**

Praise Point

Let's say yes to God.

One day Mary was alone, talking to God. Hand out the angel wings, and have children attach them to their puppets. **An angel named Gabriel appeared to her! Fly your angel through the air and say after me, "Hello, Mary! You are special. The Lord is with you."**

At first Mary was afraid. Show me how you look when you are afraid. But then the angel said to her, "Don't be afraid, Mary. God loves you. You are going to have a baby and his name will be Jesus. He will be the Son of God!" Have children remove their angel puppets' wings.

Mary answered, "I am the Lord's servant. I will do whatever God wants." Then Mary danced and sang for joy. She praised God for letting her become the mother of the Savior. Mary said yes to God. Have children make their puppets dance.

Say: **Let's be like Mary and say yes to God! When we do what God wants, it gives us joy and happiness. When I tell you an action to do, say, "I'll say yes to God!" Then dance with your puppet to tell God you say yes.** Give children an instruction, then have them say, "I'll say yes to God!" and dance with their puppets. Say:

- **God says to obey your parents.**
- **God says to be kind to others.**
- **God says to share your toys with your friends.**
- **God says to always tell the truth.**

Then hand out the puppet angel wings, and have the children attach them. Say the following rhyme, modeled after the rhyme in the book *Goodnight Moon*.

Repeat it a few times with the children and encourage them to make up actions with their puppets.

I see the angel,

And the angel sees me.

God bless the angel,

And God bless me!

Hello, Angel.

Hello, me.

Goodbye, Angel.

Goodbye from me!

Ask:

- **How did Mary say yes to God?**
- **Why did she say yes?**
- **How can we say yes to God?**
- **Why does it make God happy when we say yes to him?**

Power Prayer

Dear Jesus, we want to be like Mary and say yes to you. Please help us do the right things. Help us to do things that make you happy, like obeying our parents and being kind to others. We love you and want to serve you, the way Mary did.

Away in a Manger

Jesus Is Born

LUKE 2:1-20

Power Words

"For God so loved the world that he gave his one and only Son" (John 3:16a).

Provisions

Before class:

• Wash and dry one potato for each child.

• Cut an old bedsheet or inexpensive fabric into pieces. Each piece should be large enough to wrap a potato.

• Gather enough shoe boxes (child-sized if possible) for each child to have one. If you need to, ask a shoe store to donate its extras.

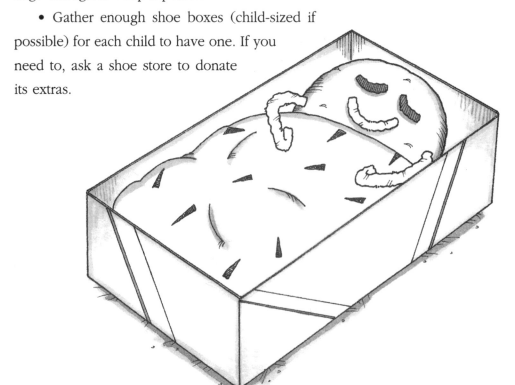

• Make a "stable" out of a large appliance box by cutting a door in one of the long sides and a window on each short end. You'll also need a string of white Christmas lights for stars, and a tray.

• Bring a Bible to class.

• Cue a cassette tape or CD to a powerful Christmas worship song such as the "Hallelujah Chorus" from Handel's *Messiah*.

For each child, you will need:
• a potato
• chenille wires
• safety scissors
• a shoe box
• craft straw
• a piece of fabric for a blanket

Puppet Pointer If a large appliance box isn't available, use a table instead. Have children go underneath the table to use as a stable.

Prepare It

Gather the children around the table. Explain to them that they will make baby Jesus puppets to help them tell the story about the day that Jesus was born.

Have each child choose a potato. Show kids how to make puppet arms by cutting a chenille wire in half and poking the wires into the sides of the potato. Have children bend the tips of the exposed wires in about a quarter of an inch to hide the sharp ends. Using three small bits of chenille wire, show children how to bend them into U shapes and stick the wire into the potato to form a mouth and eyes. Insert just the tips of the wires, then bend the U shape down, pressing it flat against the potato (see illustration). The wires will form closed "sleeping" eyes and a smiling mouth. You can also have children use markers to draw the features if you want.

Have children set their finished puppets on a tray, and put them near the stable.

Proclaim It

Set the stable somewhere in the room away from the story area and near an electrical outlet. Lay the string of Christmas lights on top of the box, and plug them in. Have the shoe boxes and tray of puppets nearby.

Set the fabric pieces in the story area. Gather children in the story area, open your Bible to Luke 2, and show it to the children.

Say: **Long ago the king wanted to count all the people living in his country. The king told the people to go to their hometowns so that he could count all of them. So Joseph and Mary saddled up their donkey and got ready to go to Bethlehem. This was going to be a hard journey because Mary was expecting a baby. Let's pretend to be Mary and Joseph and get ready for the journey. Be sure to pack something for the baby when he's born!** Hand children each a piece of fabric, and have them pretend to pack other things. Then lead them around the room, ending up near the stable.

Finally, they reached Bethlehem. They were tired. And Mary was ready to have her baby! Everywhere they went the hotels were full. No one had a room for them to sleep in. Finally, one innkeeper let them stay in his stable. Here it is! It's really a place for animals, but at least it's clean and warm and dry. Mary made a warm, dry, cozy bed for her baby in the animals' manger. Let's help Mary get the manger ready for baby Jesus.

Hand out shoe boxes with straw for the children to line the boxes with. As they work explain what a manger is and that Mary, Joseph, and Jesus probably shared the stable with several animals. Then have the children put their puppets in the shoe box mangers. Have as many children as possible sit inside the stable. If your class is large, have children take turns.

Praise Point

Jesus is God's Son.

Say: **Finally, baby Jesus was born! Hold your puppet up for everyone to see! Mary and Joseph were very proud of baby Jesus. Show how proud they looked. Wave your puppet's hand to say hello to the world.**

It was cold, so Mary wrapped baby Jesus in cloths to keep him nice and warm. Have children "unpack" the fabric they were given earlier and wrap Jesus in it while you finish the story.

While this was happening, the Bible says that an angel appeared to some shepherds nearby. The angel said, "Don't be afraid! I bring you good news! Today a Savior has been born; he is Christ the Lord. You will find him wrapped in cloths and lying in a manger." Then lots of angels appeared and sang praises to God. The shepherds went to find baby Jesus. They praised him and worshipped him. Then they went and told everyone the great news that the Savior was born.

Praise & Play With It

Say: **Let's put our baby Jesus puppets in the stable. We'll pretend to be the shepherds and worship him because he is God's Son.**

Have children walk around the room pretending to be the shepherds taking care of their sheep. Explain that the angels were so bright and beautiful that the shepherds were terrified of them at first. At intervals turn on the Christmas praise music. When children hear the music, have them fall down and pretend to be afraid like the shepherds were. When you turn the music off, have kids say, "Jesus is God's Son!" Repeat the activity a few times.

Then have children go to the stable and pick up their puppets.

Say: **When the shepherds found baby Jesus in the manger, they were amazed. They worshipped him and were very happy. Today when we celebrate Jesus' birthday, we worship him too. Let's use our puppets to worship Jesus for being God's Son.**

Briefly talk with children about ways to praise God, such as praying quietly, praying aloud, singing, clapping, dancing, bowing down, and moving around in a joyful way.

We can praise God in many ways. Think of a way for you and your puppet to praise Jesus for being God's Son. When I tell you something great about Jesus, you and your puppet say, "Jesus is God's Son" and show us a way to worship him.

Say things such as "Jesus heals people," "Jesus forgives our sins," "Jesus helps us," "Jesus rose from the dead," and "Jesus loves us." Then have kids and their puppets worship God. If you want, have children do it one at a time, and have them lead everyone else in worship.

 Puppet Pointer Keep the stable set up for the next puppet lesson about the wise men.

Talk About It

Ask:

- **What did the angels tell the shepherds?**
- **What did the shepherds do when they saw Jesus?**
- **Why do we worship Jesus?**
- **What are ways we worship Jesus?**

Power Prayer

God, thank you for sending Jesus. Help us always to worship you, Jesus, because you are God's Son. We believe in you. We love you.

Wise Tracks

The Wise Kings

MATTHEW 2:1-12

Power Words

"Come, let us bow down in worship" (Psalm 95:6a).

Provisions

Before class:

• Use the stable constructed for the previous lesson, "Away in a Manger" (p. 67). If you don't have a box, use a table for the children to sit under, and set it up near an electrical outlet. Set a string of white Christmas lights on the tabletop for stars. Wrap a doll in a blanket, and set it inside the stable. Put a flashlight in the story area.

• Cut full-size sheets of poster board in half. About six to eight inches down from the top of a short edge, cut an oval the size of a child's face. Measure the poster board on an actual child so you know how large an oval you need.

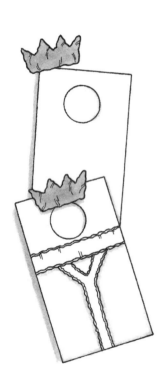

• Cut one-dimensional crowns from gold, silver, or holographic foil wrap to fit on top of the oval holes in the poster board.

• Bring a Bible to class.

For each child, you will need:

• a piece of poster board with a face hole cut out of it

• a foil paper crown

• glue and/or glitter glue

• stick-on jewels or stickers, large beads, pompoms, stickers, or other decorative items

Prepare It

Gather the children around the table. Explain to them that *they* will be the special puppets today to tell the story of wise kings who searched for Jesus.

Give each child a sheet of poster board with a face hole cut out of it. Help each child choose a crown and glue it in place. Set out the stick-on jewels, glitter glue, or other craft supplies you brought, and let children decorate their crowns. They can also draw robes and decorate the clothing if they want.

Proclaim It

Turn on the Christmas lights over the stable. Gather children in the story area with their king puppet masks. Set a chair in the area for Herod's throne, and have the flashlight near you. Open your Bible to Matthew 2, and show it to the children.

Say: **After Jesus was born in Bethlehem, wise kings from a faraway land came looking for him. I see I have some very royal-looking kings in class today! Let's make groups of three to act out our story.** Help children arrange themselves in trios and spread out around the room. Tell them to listen carefully and act out your instructions while holding up their masks. Turn the classroom lights off and the flashlight on, and hold it in the air as you continue. Ask for a volunteer to be Mary, and tell her to go to the stable and hold the baby doll when you tell her.

The wise kings saw the special star in the sky. Point to the bright star. They knew that the bright star meant the Savior was born. The kings got on their camels and traveled to see King Herod. Travel with your group now, and go to King Herod's throne in the story area. Sit on the king's throne, and continue the story.

When they arrived, the wise kings asked King Herod, "Where is the baby we are looking for? He is a king."

King Herod was upset. He didn't want anyone to be king but himself. But he said, "Go and look for the child. When you find him, come and tell me so I can worship him too." But he didn't really want to worship the baby, he wanted to get rid of the baby.

So the wise kings set out on their journey again to find the new king. The star went ahead of them, and they followed it until it stopped over the place where the child was. **Let's follow the star to find the king.** Still holding the flashlight up, lead the children around the room. Stop a few times, shine the light, and pretend to look for Jesus inside places—drawers, cupboards, and toy boxes, for example. Announce that he's not there, then continue on to the stable. When you get to the stable, set the flashlight on the roof of the stable. Have the Mary volunteer hold the doll.

Praise Point

God wants us to worship Jesus.

The kings finally arrived in Bethlehem, where the star was shining brightly over the place where Jesus was. The wise kings were filled with joy. **Show me how they looked.**

When they saw the child with his mother Mary, they bowed down and worshipped him. Then they gave treasures and special gifts to him. **Let's bow down and pretend to give Jesus gifts.**

Later the wise kings were warned in a dream not to go back to Herod. So they went home another way.

Praise & Play With It

Hide the baby Jesus doll somewhere in the room. Have children stay in groups of three. Give each group a chance to shine the flashlight and find the hidden baby before the rest of the class finishes saying (or singing) the following rhyme. If a group hasn't found it by the end of the song, tell the group where to find it. Hide the baby again, and let a new group find the baby.

Starlight, star bright,

Brightest star I see tonight.

Pray I may, pray I might

Find the Savior of the world tonight.

Talk About It

Ask:

- **What were the wise kings looking for?**
- **Why were they looking for him?**
- **How can you worship Jesus?**
- **What gifts can you give Jesus?**

Power Prayer

Jesus, you are the Savior of the world! You are the King of Kings and the Lord of Lords. We give you all our love. It's our best gift. We love you and worship you.

Go Fish!

Fishers of Men

LUKE 5:4-11

Power Words

"Come, follow me...and I will make you fishers of men" (Matthew 4:19).

Provisions

Puppet Pointer For an alternative to glow-in-the-dark paints, use glow-in-the-dark crayons, chalk, markers, or stickers.

Before class:

• Cut large fish shapes out of different colored poster board. The fish should be about 10x15 inches. Tape each fish to a twenty-four-inch long dowel.

• Purchase a fishnet at a party or craft store.

• Use masking tape to make an outline of a boat on your floor.

• Bring a Bible and a pair of scissors to class.

For each child, you will need:

- a fish shape on a dowel
- glow-in-the-dark paints
- a paintbrush
- blue and green curling ribbon or crepe paper
- markers, gel pens, or glitter glue

Prepare It

Gather the children around the table. Explain to them that they will make special fish puppets to help tell the story about something special Jesus told his friends to do.

Have each child choose a fish shape and use the glow-in-the-dark paints to decorate them. Allow children to also use the markers and other supplies if available. As the children work, cut green and blue curling ribbon or crepe paper into varying lengths, about twenty-four to thirty-six inches long. Curl the ribbon slightly, and tie some of each color to the dowel immediately under the fish.

Proclaim It

Set the fishnet in the middle of the masking-tape outline of the boat. Gather children in the story area with their fish puppets. Open your Bible to Luke 5, and show it to the children.

Say: **When Jesus started teaching the people about the way to heaven, he chose twelve people to be his special helpers. They were called disciples. He gave his disciples a special job to do. Let's find out what that job was. Every time you hear me use a word that has "fish" in it, raise your fish up in the air, and wiggle it back and forth.**

Simon was a <u>fisherman</u>. He had a <u>fishing</u> boat that he used to catch his <u>fish</u>. Let's pretend we're Simon and get in our <u>fishing</u> boat. Walk over to the boat outline and have everyone climb on board. **Is everyone in the boat? We don't want anyone to get wet! That night Simon and his friends worked hard and <u>fished</u> all night long. But they didn't catch any <u>fish</u>.**

The next day as they were cleaning their nets, Jesus came by. A lot of people were following him, wanting to hear him teach. Jesus asked Simon if he could use his boat for a while. "Yes," said Simon. So Jesus got into the boat and pushed it out a little from shore. Jesus sat down and taught the

Jesus wants us to tell others about him.

people from the boat. That way everyone could see him and hear him.

Afterward, Jesus thanked Simon. Then he said, "Simon, put your boat out into that deep water over there and put down your nets to catch some <u>fish</u>."

Simon answered, "Teacher, we worked hard all night and didn't catch one <u>fish</u>. But because you say so, we'll try one more time." So Simon and his friends rowed to the spot where Jesus told them. Then they put down their nets. Throw the <u>fishnet</u> overboard. **Suddenly, things went wild! Their net was full of wet, wiggly, wonderful <u>fish</u>! In fact there were so many <u>fish</u> that Simon needed more people to come and help him! The boats were filled with so many <u>fish</u> that they began to sink!**

When Simon saw this, he and his friends knew that Jesus was powerful. They wanted to follow him. Jesus said, "From now on you will catch men, not <u>fish</u>." Jesus meant that he wanted them to tell people about him. So the men pulled their boats up on shore. They left everything behind and they followed Jesus.

Praise & Play With It

Say: **Jesus wants us to tell others about him too. He wants us to "fish" for people, just as his friends did. That's the special job he gave his disciples. It's also the job he gives us. Let's play a game to tell Jesus that we'll share his love with others.**

Have one or two children at a time sit inside the boat outline. Have the other children lie on the floor around the boat with their puppets. Sing the following rhyme to the tune of "Row, Row, Row Your Boat." As you sing, have the children in the boat drop the net overboard. On the last phrase, the children on the floor should raise their fish up near the side of the boat, wiggle them, then lay them inside the boat outline.

For extra fun, serve gummy fish as a snack, and have children name people that they want to share Jesus' love with.

Row, row, row your boat.
Drop your net in now!
I'll share his love with everyone
And tell his name to all.

Repeat the game several times.

Pin or tape the fishnet to a bulletin board or wall. Place it as low as possible so it's at child-height. Have children name people they want to tell about Jesus, then put their fish in the net.

Talk About It

Ask:

- **What happened when Simon put his nets where Jesus told him?**
- **What new job did Jesus give Simon and his friends?**
- **Why does Jesus want us to tell others about him?**
- **Who will you share Jesus' love with?**

Power Prayer

Jesus, we praise you because you are God. You told Simon to fish for men. We want to do that too, Jesus. Help us to tell others about you. Help us to share your love. We love you, Jesus!

A Dark and Stormy Night

The Storm at Sea

LUKE 8:22-25

Power Words

"Even the winds and the water…obey him" (Luke 8:25b).

Provisions

Before class:

• Fill a plastic tub with an inch or two of warm water. You will also need a towel.

• Cut people shapes and semicircular "boat" shapes from different colored craft foam. The people shapes should be about three inches high; the boats, about two or three inches high and at least six inches long. To make the people, you can pho-tocopy the pattern in the

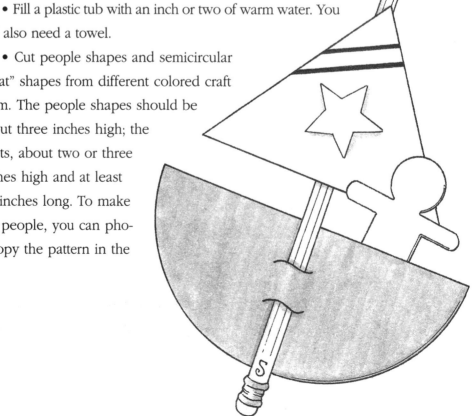

margin, enlarge it to the right proportions, cut it out, and trace the shape on the foam.

- Cut two slits, one above the other, on one side of each boat.
- Using different colors of paper, cut triangles for sails.
- Put a pillow or cushion in the story area.
- Bring a Bible to class.

For each child, you will need:
- a foam boat shape
- a foam person shape
- a self-adhesive Velcro circle
- an unsharpened pencil
- a paper triangle
- tape
- permanent markers or pens (optional)

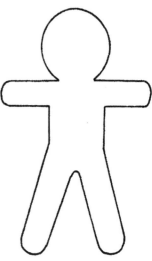

 Prepare It

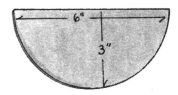

Gather the children around the table. Explain to them that they will make special puppets to help them tell a story about how Jesus is stronger than anything.

Have each child choose a boat shape and a person shape. Help each one peel the adhesive off the Velcro circle and put one of the pieces on the front of the boat shape at the end opposite the slits. Help them place the other Velcro piece on the person in a location that positions the figure inside the boat when attached—on the back of the leg, for example.

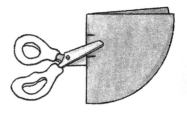

Help each child slide an unsharpened pencil up through the slits and tape a paper triangle to the top of it for a sail. The bottom of the pencil is the puppet handle. Then give children time to decorate their boats and people, if desired.

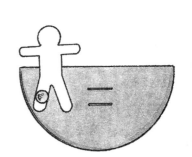

 Proclaim It

Gather the children in the story area with their boat and people puppets. Have them separate the Velcro circle pieces. Open your Bible to Luke 8, and show it to the children.

Say: **Jesus is bigger and stronger than anything. Let's hear a story from the Bible that tells about an amazing thing Jesus did to prove this.**

One day Jesus said to his disciples, "Let's go over to the other side of

Jesus is stronger than anything.

the lake." So everyone got in the boat to go to the other side. Put your puppet inside your boat.

As they sailed, Jesus fell asleep on a cushion in the back of the boat. Lie back on the pillow and pretend to sleep, then continue. **Suddenly a terrible storm came upon them. The wind was blowing and the waves were huge. The tiny boat tossed and turned. Show me how your boat would look in the storm.**

Soon the boat filled with water. The disciples were in great danger. They were terrified. They woke Jesus up and said, "Teacher, Teacher, we're going to drown!" Keep your boats tossing about in the storm.

Jesus got up. Stand up. **He spoke loudly to the wind and waves, "Quiet! Be still!"** Wait until children stop their boats, then continue in a whisper. **The storm stopped just as quickly as it had started. All was calm and quiet.** Continue in a normal tone of voice.

The disciples were amazed. They wondered about Jesus—who was this man that even the wind and waves obeyed him? Can you help the disciples with their questions? Who was Jesus, and why did the wind and waves obey him?

Praise & Play With It

Set the tub of warm water on a towel on top of a table. If your class is large, use more than one tub. Gather the children around the tub with their puppets. Have them remove the pencil sails and separate the people from the boats.

Say: **Jesus saved the disciples on the lake by making the storm go away. He can do that because he is God. Jesus is stronger than anything! Let's use our boats and puppets to praise God for being so strong.**

Have children experiment floating their boats on the water (laying them flat), then sticking them to the sides of the tub when they're wet. Have them add their disciples to their boats. After a few minutes, have them lay their boats, without the figures, flat in the water.

Sing the following rhyme to the tune of "The Eency Weency Spider." When you sing about the storm, make waves by gently swirling the water with your hand. When you sing about Jesus, attach the people, stand the boats upright, and press them against the side of the tub.

The eency weency boat
Went out to sail the sea.

Along came the wind
And blew the boat about!

Up Jesus woke
And chased the storm away.
And the eency weency boat
Sailed safely home that day.

Tell children to use their puppets in the tub at home and to practice telling the story about Jesus calming the storm. Remind them that Jesus can do anything.

 Talk About It

Ask:

- **Why were the disciples afraid?**
- **How did Jesus help the disciples?**
- **What are some things you're afraid of?**
- **How does Jesus help you?**

Power Prayer

Jesus, you are stronger than anything! Help us to trust you when we're afraid. Thank you for your promise to help. We love you, Lord.

Free Lunch

Feeding the Five Thousand

JOHN 6:1-13

Power Words

"All things are possible with God" (Mark 10:27b).

Provisions

Before class:

• Cut a U-shaped flap in the center of the back of each paper lunch sack. The flap should be about three inches up from the bottom of the sack and large enough for a child's hand to fit inside.

• Cut circles out of construction paper for puppet heads.

• Bring a Bible and a large bowl to class.

For each child, you will need:

- a paper lunch sack
- markers
- several pretzel nuggets
- several fish-shaped crackers
- a construction-paper circle
- access to a stapler

Prepare It

Gather the children around the table. Explain to them that they will make special puppets to help tell the story about Jesus using a little boy's lunch for something very special.

Give each child a lunch sack. Help each child staple the bag shut and staple or glue the paper circle "head" to the top of the bag. Have him or her decorate the front of the bag to look like a little boy.

Proclaim It

Set out five pretzels and two fish-shaped crackers for each child. Gather children in the story area with their puppets. Tell children not to eat the crackers or pretzels. Open your Bible to John 6, and show it to the children.

Say: **One day a little boy took his lunch and went to hear Jesus teach. Make your little boy puppet say, "Teach me, Jesus."**

The little boy followed the crowds and squeezed his way to the front. The little boy wanted to be close to Jesus so he could hear and see everything. Walk your puppet like he's going to see Jesus.

Jesus taught for a long time. He healed many people. It was getting late, and the people had not had anything to eat.

Jesus said to his disciples, "You give them something to eat."

"What?" they asked. "How can we feed so many? If we worked for eight months, we wouldn't have enough to buy bread for all of them!"

But one of Jesus' friends named Andrew had met the little boy. Shake hands with your neighbor to show that Andrew and the boy knew each other. Andrew knew that the boy had brought a lunch. So he said to Jesus, "Here is a boy with five small barley loaves and two small fish. But that's not enough for this many." Put two fish crackers and five pretzels inside your bag.

Jesus took the lunch—even though it was so small. The little boy knew Jesus could do anything! He was happy to give Jesus his lunch. Let's pretend to give our lunches to Jesus the way the little boy gave his lunch to Jesus. Set an empty bowl in the center of the story area, and have them put the snacks from their bags into the bowl.

Then something amazing happened. Jesus took the little boy's lunch and told everyone to sit down. Hold up the bowl. **Then he thanked God for the food and began to feed everyone.** Pass out a handful of the snacks to each child to eat. **Can you guess what happened? There was enough bread and fish for everyone to eat as much as they wanted! When everyone was full, they collected the leftovers so that nothing would be wasted. They collected twelve baskets full! And all from one little boy's lunch! Jesus can do anything!**

Say: **Jesus can do anything. He took the little boy's lunch and fed five thousand people with it! God wants to use you, too. You're never too little to do things for God.** Brainstorm with children some things that God wants them to do. If they need help, suggest such things as sharing their toys, obeying their parents, giving hugs, and being kind to one another.

Let's use our puppets to praise Jesus because he can do anything. I'm going to tell you things that are little. You scrunch down with your puppet really little. Wait until you hear me say that Jesus turns it into something big. Then you jump up big and tall and make your puppet say, "Jesus can do anything!" in a big loud voice. Are you ready?

Say things such as the following, and give children time to respond.

• **The little boy gave his little lunch to Jesus. Jesus turned it into a great big lunch!**

• **You give your mom or dad a little kiss. Jesus turns it into a great big happy feeling!**

• **We plant a little seed. Jesus turns it into a great big tree!**

• **A little baby is born. Jesus turns it into a great big person!**

• **You treat your friend with a little bit of kindness. Jesus turns it into a great big friendship!**

Talk About It

Ask:

- **What did the little boy give to Jesus?**

- **What happened to the little boy's lunch?**

- **What can you give to Jesus?**

- **How can Jesus help you when you give those things?**

Power Prayer

Jesus, we praise you because you can do anything! Help us to do the things you want us to do. Help us to obey our parents, share our toys, and be kind to our friends. Thank you that we're never too little to do something for you. We love you so much, Jesus.

Walking on Water

Jesus Walks on Water

MATTHEW 14:22-33

"Yours, O Lord, is the greatness and the power" (1 Chronicles 29:11a).

Before class:

• Cut a small slit or hole big enough to fit the "legs" of a clothespin into the center of each large sponge.

• Cut additional sponges into small pieces, approximately 1½x1¾ inches.

• Fill a tub with an inch or two of warm water. Have two towels on hand.

• Bring a Bible to class.

For each child, you will need:

- a sponge with a slit cut in the center
- a non-spring clothespin
- permanent markers
- a small sponge piece

Prepare It

Gather the children around the table. Explain to them that they will make special puppets to tell the story about Jesus walking on water.

Give each child a clothespin, and have him or her draw a face on the head of it to represent Jesus. To represent Peter, have each child draw a face on a small piece of sponge.

Proclaim It

Set the tub of warm water on a towel in the story area. Cover it with another towel until you need it for the story. Have the large sponges nearby. Have the children sit in the story area with their clothespins and small sponge puppets. Open your Bible to Matthew 14, and show it to the children.

Say: **Our Bible story today comes from the book of Matthew. It tells about an amazing thing that Jesus did to show how powerful he is. The characters in our story are Peter—hold up your sponge puppet and say hi to Peter—and Jesus. Hold up your clothespin puppet and say hello to Jesus.**

One evening after teaching all day, Jesus sent his friends ahead of him across the lake, while he sent the crowd of people home. He wanted to go to a quiet place by himself to pray. So the disciples went down to the lake and set out in their boat. Let's pretend to row our boat as they did. Pretend to row a boat.

Uncover the tub of water, and insert your clothespin into the hole of a large sponge as you say the following: **Before long, a big wind came up. The waters got wild and rough.** Have everyone rock their bodies back and forth. **They were having a hard time rowing. Jesus knew the boat was in trouble, so he went out to it. Only he didn't use a boat. He walked on top of the water!** Set your puppet on the water, and gently push it from one side of the tub to the other while you continue.

When the disciples saw him walking on the water, they were scared.

But Jesus said, "Don't be afraid! It's me—Jesus!" Hold up your Peter puppet.

Jesus is powerful.

Peter was excited. He was amazed that Jesus was walking on the water. He wanted to do it too. He said, "Lord, if it's you, tell me to come to you on the water."

So Jesus said, "Come." Set your Peter puppet on the sponge with Jesus.

So Peter got out of the boat. He walked on the water toward Jesus! But then he got afraid and started to sink in the water. Tip Peter into the water. He cried out, "Help, Lord, save me!"

Jesus caught him right away. Pick Peter up, and put him back on the sponge. "Why did you get afraid and doubt, Peter?" Then they both climbed into the boat.

What do you think happened to the storm? It died down and went away. What do you think everyone in the boat was thinking? They all worshipped Jesus saying, "Truly, you are the Son of God." Now it's your turn to make Jesus walk on water.

Pass out the large sponges, and show the children how to insert a Jesus puppet into a sponge to make it stand up. Give everyone a chance to float their Jesus and Peter puppets. Have several children retell parts of the story as they play.

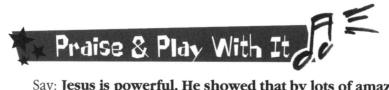

Praise & Play With It

Say: **Jesus is powerful. He showed that by lots of amazing things he did. Besides walking on water, by what other ways did Jesus show he is powerful?** Prompt children to recall the stories about Jesus calming the storm and feeding five thousand people.

Set the tub of water on the floor. Have children hold their clothespin puppets and stand in a circle around the tub.

Say: **Jesus is powerful. He walked on water to show his disciples that he is God. Let's use our puppets to praise Jesus because he's powerful. When it's your turn, say something good about Jesus, like "Jesus is great!" or "Jesus is powerful!" Then toss your clothespin into the tub of water.**

Have children take turns saying praise statements and tossing their clothespins in the water. When everyone has had a turn, have everyone clap and say, "Yea, Jesus is powerful!" Point out to the children that their puppets float even without the sponges.

If there's time, allow children to play in the water with their puppets. Remind them to use their puppets in their bathtubs at home and to tell their families the story about Jesus walking on water.

Ask:

- **What did Jesus do in the story?**
- **Why did Peter start sinking in the water?**
- **How do we know Jesus is powerful?**
- **How does Jesus help you?**

Power Prayer

Jesus, you are the most powerful person of all. We praise you because you are powerful. You prove you are God by helping us. Thank you, Jesus. We love you.

Good Neighbors

The Good Samaritan

LUKE 10:25-37

Power Words

"Be kind…to one another" (Ephesians 4:32a).

Provisions

Before class:

• Purchase one sticker for each child. If possible, find stickers that say or represent something about being good helpers or being kind, such as hearts or stars. They need to be small enough to fit on the 4x6-inch puppets.

• Bring a Bible to class.

For each child, you will need:

- two 4x6 index cards
- access to a stapler
- a chenille wire
- markers
- several bandages
- red, blue, and brown crayons
- several other colors of crayons
- a sticker

 Prepare It

Gather the children around the table. Explain to them that they will make special puppets to help tell a story about being kind to others.

Give children two index cards apiece, and help them staple the cards on the edges, about halfway up. Have each child insert a chenille wire between the two cards for arms (fold the chenille wires in, hiding the sharp tips), then continue stapling the edges around the top. Leave the bottom end open, creating a pocket for children to slide their hands into. Have children use markers to draw faces and hair on their puppets. On one side, they should draw a smiling face; on the other, they should draw a frowning face with closed eyes.

Puppet Pointer If you don't want to make arms out of chenille wire, use strips of construction paper folded accordion style.

 Proclaim It

Gather children in the story area with their people puppets. Have the crayons and bandages near you. Open your Bible to Luke 10, and show it to the children.

Puppet Pointer If you don't have enough crayons, have children work in pairs or trios and share them.

Say: **One time a man said to Jesus, "I know the Bible says I should love God. It also says I should love my neighbor, but who is my neighbor?"**

Jesus answered the man by telling him a story. I'm going to tell you that story now. Your puppets will help you remember the story. Give each child a blue, red, and brown crayon.

Once there was a man walking down a road. Put your hand inside your puppet and make him walk down the road. Good job!

91

Suddenly bad guys jumped out at him. They knocked him down. They took his money and clothes and everything he owned. Lay your puppet down so just his sad face is showing. His eyes are closed. They hurt him very badly. Take your blue crayons and draw some tears on his face.

Now use your red crayon and draw some "owies" on him. Use your brown crayon to make some dirt spots on him to show how dirty he got when they threw him on the ground.

Set your crayons on the floor while we tell the rest of our story. We'll need them again in a minute. A little while later, a man came down the road. He was a worker in God's Temple. Maybe he would help the hurt man. But he didn't! He walked right by the man and didn't help him one little bit. Walk your fingers past your hurting puppet.

Soon another person came by. But he didn't stop to help either! Walk your fingers past your puppet in the other direction.

A little while later, a man on a donkey came clip-clopping by. He was from another country. This man stopped when he saw the hurt man. He cleaned him up and put bandages on his hurt places. Hand a few bandages to the children to put on their puppets.

Then the man gave him clothes to wear and took him to an inn where he could rest and get better. Turn your puppet to the happy side to show that the man felt better. Use your crayons now to color new clothes on him. Set out other crayons for the children to use. As they work continue the story.

When Jesus finished telling the story, he asked the man a question. "Who was a neighbor to the hurt man?" What would you answer to that question?

Of course, the answer is the one who helped him. Jesus wants us to learn that we can be a neighbor to anyone who needs our help. Put your hand inside your puppet now. Use your happy side puppet to say hi to your neighbor. Tell your neighbor, "Jesus wants us to be kind to others."

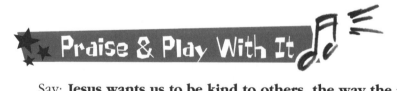

Say: **Jesus wants us to be kind to others, the way the man in our story was. What are some ways you can be kind to others?**

Let's play a game to remind us to be kind. When I come to you and take your hand, tell me one way you can be kind to someone this week. Then

I'll put a special helper's sticker on your puppet's robe. Then we'll go together to find someone else.

Go to a child, and have him or her share a way to be kind to someone. Put a sticker on his or her puppet, and set the puppet aside for the child to take home later. Take the child's hand and go to another child. Continue until every child is given a sticker and has joined the group.

Ask:

- **What happened to the man when he was walking down the road?**
- **Which man was the good neighbor?**
- **Why does Jesus want us to be kind to others?**
- **What are some ways you can be kind?**

Power Prayer

Jesus, thank you for showing us how to be kind. Help us to be kind to our family and friends. Help us to be kind to everyone smaller than us. We're never too big or too little to be kind. Thank you, Jesus. We love you.

The Little Lost Sheep

The Lost Sheep

LUKE 15:1-7

★ Power Words

"I am the good shepherd; I know my sheep and my sheep know me" (John 10:14).

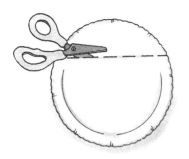

★ Provisions

Before class:

• Cut off a third of each small paper plate for each child.

• Pour glue into bowls or empty margarine tubs, and dilute the glue with a little bit of water.

• Cut black felt into rectangles, circles, and triangles. For each child, you'll need two rectangles for legs, two circles for eyes, and two triangles for ears (see illustration).

94

- Practice the story so that you can say it without reading the script.
- Bring a Bible to class.

For each child, you will need:
- two small white paper plates (one cut and one uncut)
- access to a stapler
- glue
- a paintbrush
- fiberfill or cotton balls
- set of black felt shapes

Prepare It

Gather the children around the table. Explain to them that they will make sheep puppets to help tell the story about a sheep that was lost.

Give each child two paper plates, one cut and one uncut. Help each child staple the two plates together with the tops of the plates facing each other to the inside. Leave the cut edge unstapled. This will form a pocket for the child to insert his or her hand into.

Set the plates cut-side down on the table, with the unstapled edge at the bottom. Help children staple or glue two black rectangles for legs at the bottom center of the plate and hanging off the plate.

When the legs are in place, have the children use a paintbrush to cover the plate with glue. While the glue is still wet, have them gently press small amounts of cotton or fiberfill on the plate until it's completely covered. Have children glue on two black felt circles for the eyes and two black triangles for the ears.

Proclaim It

Make sure there is a chair in the story area. Gather children around you with their sheep puppets. Open your Bible to Luke 15, and show it to the children.

Say: **Our story comes from the book of Luke. Jesus told a story about a shepherd who had one hundred sheep. That's a lot of sheep! Wiggle your sheep at me and say, "Baa!" Now say it louder so you sound like one hundred sheep! Good job!**

Jesus said that if one little sheep got lost, the shepherd would leave all the others and search the countryside until he found that one sheep. Jesus

said that's how important we are to him. **Let's tell the story of the lost sheep in a fun way.**

Line the children up holding their sheep puppets, and move down the line as you tell this story in the style of "This Little Piggy."

This little sheep was first in line. Touch the first child and the puppet on their heads.

This little sheep was next. Touch the second.

This little sheep played a twirling game. Turn the child around in a circle.

This little sheep did not. Touch the child and the puppet on their heads.

And *this* little sheep ran away and got lost! Gently pull the child away from the group, and sit him or her in the chair.

The shepherd called the sheep: Here sheep, sheep, sheep, sheep, sheep! Pause briefly.

This little sheep came running. Touch the heads of the next child and puppet in line.

This little sheep started walking. Touch the next heads.

This little sheep went skipping. Touch the next heads.

And this little sheep did not! Touch the next heads, then go over to the chair.

And *this* little sheep went baa, baa, baa, baa because he [or she] **was lost!** Touch the heads of the child and the puppet in the chair.

The shepherd called the little lost sheep: Here I come to find you!

The shepherd came running. Run in place.

And scooped the little sheep up! Gently pull the child off the chair.

And he held it and hugged it all-l-l the way home! Hug the child, and put him or her at the front of the line.

Repeat the game until everyone has been included. Encourage the children to try saying the story with you.

Say: **Jesus told that story because he wants us to know that he is the good shepherd. He wants you to know that you are as important to him as that lost sheep. So if you ever feel afraid or lost, remember that Jesus knows where you are. He'll keep you safe and protect you.**

Praise & Play With It

Say: **Jesus is the good shepherd. He always knows where we are. With him we are never lost. Let's play a game to thank Jesus for that.**

Have a child hide his or her sheep puppet somewhere in the room, while the rest of the children cover their eyes with their puppets. Then have everyone search for the hidden puppet. When the puppet is found, have everyone say, "Jesus always knows where we are."

Repeat the game, letting other children hide their puppets. If your class is large, have two or more children hide their puppets at a time.

Talk About It

Ask:

- **What happened to the little sheep?**
- **What did the good shepherd do?**
- **How is Jesus like that shepherd?**
- **How does it make you feel to know that Jesus always knows where you are?**

Power Prayer

Jesus, thank you for being our good shepherd. Thank you that you always know where we are. Help us to talk to you when we feel scared or lost. You are always with us. We love you, Jesus!

Jesus Loves Me

Jesus and the Children

MARK 10:13-16

"Let the little children come to me" (Mark 10:14b).

Before class:

• Purchase 1½-inch diameter wooden craft spools (about two-inches high) and twelve-inch wooden dowels from a craft store. The dowels need to be small enough in diameter to fit inside the hole of the spool.

• Purchase chenille wire and curly craft hair or craft feathers.

• Cut a variety of fabric scraps about half the height of a wooden spool and long enough to wrap around a spool.

• Recruit an adult helper to play the part of Jesus during the Bible story. Let him read the story in the "Proclaim It" section so he knows what to say and when.

• Bring a Bible to class.

For each child, you will need:

• a wooden craft spool

• a wooden dowel

• tape

• fabric

• glue

• markers

• a chenille wire

• curly craft hair or a small craft feather

Prepare It

Gather the children around the table. Explain to them that they will make special puppets to help them tell a story about children visiting Jesus.

Give each child a spool, and have him or her cover one of the holes with tape. This will be the top of the puppet's head. Have him or her choose fabric and glue it around the bottom half of the spool's side and then add eyes, nose, and a mouth with markers.

Help each child wrap a chenille wire around the puppet's body to make arms. Start at the front of the puppet by placing the middle of the chenille wire at the top edge of the fabric. Wind the wire around to the back, twist it once, and bring it back around to the sides to make the arms. Bend the ends over to hide the sharp tips.

Last of all, have the children spread glue on the heads of their puppets and attach curly craft hair or craft feathers. Have them insert dowels into the spools to use as handles for their puppets.

Proclaim It

Have the adult helper get ready to play the Jesus role, and sit in an area of the room away from the story area. Gather children in the story area with their puppets. Open your Bible to Mark 10, and show it to the children.

Say: **The Bible tells a story that is very important to children. It tells**

everyone how important children are to Jesus! You and your puppets can help me act out the story. Here's what happened.

One day some mothers and their children were on their way to see Jesus. The children were happy! Show me your happy children puppets.

The mothers carried the babies while the boys and girls skipped and hopped and danced along. Some of you can pretend to be moms and dads holding your children. Some of you can be the children. Show me how everyone looked. They couldn't wait to see Jesus! Lead children around the room, ending up near the chair with "Jesus" in it. Stop the children before they get to Jesus.

When they were almost there, Jesus' friends stopped them. Stand between the children and Jesus. They told the children to go home! "Jesus is too busy to bother with you," they said.

The children were sad. Some of them cried. Show me how they looked.

But Jesus heard what was going on. Jesus was mad! He didn't want the children to leave. Jesus said…(Have Jesus say, "Don't stop them. Let the little children come to me.")

So the children all went to Jesus. Take your puppet children to Jesus. Take them off the sticks, and set them on Jesus' lap. Jesus blessed the children. He was not too busy. He loved them. Children are important to Jesus.

Praise & Play With It

Have the children gather around Jesus. Collect their dowels. Have the volunteer return the puppets to the children to use in the following activity.

Say: **Jesus wants you to always remember that you're important to him. Jesus loves you! Let's use our puppets to thank Jesus for that.**

Have each child hold his or her own puppet. Ask Jesus to say things such as "I'm looking for someone wearing red." Have all the children wearing red or with red on their puppet stand up. Then to that group have Jesus say, "I'm looking for someone named [name a child standing]." Direct that child to go to the volunteer with his or her puppet and receive a hug. Have the person tell each child something special such as "Jesus loves you" or "You are special."

Repeat until all the children have been hugged.

Ask:

- **Where were the children going?**
- **What did Jesus' friends do when they saw the children?**
- **How did Jesus feel about that?**
- **How does Jesus feel about you?**

Power Prayer

Jesus, thank you that you love us! That makes us happy. You make us feel important, Jesus. Help us to always come to you whenever we want. We love you, Jesus.

Alive Again!

The Resurrection

JOHN 19:38–20:18

Power Words

"I am the resurrection and the life" (John 11:25a).

Provisions

Before class:

• Cut a small U-shaped opening in the top of each paper cup. When the cup is tipped upside down it, will be a "cave" with a rounded doorway. Also cut a slit in the bottom of each cup, wide enough for a craft stick to slip through.

• Collect smooth stones or rocks small enough to fit in a child's hand but large enough to cover the opening of the paper cup.

• Bring a low-heat glue gun and a Bible to class.

102

For each child, you will need:

- a paper cup with an opening and a slit cut in it
- a small rock or stone
- a wide craft stick
- markers or paints
- fabric scraps
- yarn
- safety scissors
- glue
- a cookie or other small treat

Prepare It

Gather the children around the table. Give each child a craft stick, a prepared paper cup, and a stone. Explain that each of the items will be used to help tell the story about Jesus rising from the dead.

Have each child draw a smiley face on one side of the stone and a frowning face on the other side. Ask each child to do the same to one end of the craft stick, drawing a happy person on one side and a sad person on the other. Have children decorate both sides of their craft sticks, using the fabric scraps as clothing. Allow them to cut lengths of the yarn for hair. Out of children's reach, have an adult helper use a low-heat glue gun to glue the yarn hair to the craft sticks.

Proclaim It

Gather children in the story area with their Resurrection puppets. Open your Bible to John 19, and show it to the children.

Say: **Jesus did many amazing and wonderful things while he lived on earth. Best of all, he showed people what God, his Father, was like. He told everyone how to get to heaven. This made some people very happy. Hold your craft-stick person up and show me the happy side. Jesus' friends loved him and followed him. Make your puppet dance to show how happy they were to know and follow Jesus.**

Some people got mad when Jesus told them they were doing bad things. Show me your frowning-face stick puppet. They hated Jesus so much that they wanted to hurt him. Hold your frowning puppet up higher.

But still many others turned from being bad and started believing in

Jesus. They started doing good things that made them happy. Let's hold up our happy stick puppets again.

Jesus' enemies finally arrested him and put him on a cross. That was a very sad day. Show me your sad puppets crying. Jesus' friends were scared and sad. Their best friend and teacher was gone.

They took him down from the cross, wrapped him in white cloth, and laid him in a tomb that was in a garden nearby. A tomb is a place where people are buried. Jesus' tomb was sort of like a cave. Take your paper cup and set it upside down to make the tomb. A great big, huge stone was rolled in front of the cave so no one could get in. Put your stone in front of the door with the sad face showing.

Now stand your sad puppet next to the tomb. Let's be really still and quiet for a moment. For three long days everyone was sad and quiet without Jesus. Pause and wait until everyone is quiet, then continue in a quiet voice, gradually getting louder.

Now take your stone, and lay it next to the tomb with the smiley side up because something wonderful happened next. One of Jesus' friends named Mary came to the tomb. She was still feeling sad. Pretend your sad stick puppet is Mary, and walk her to the tomb. When she got to the tomb she was surprised. The stone was rolled away from the entrance. She looked inside. Have the puppets look inside. What did she see in there? Nothing! That's what she saw. Jesus was gone! Is your tomb empty?

Mary ran to her friends (have the puppets run in place) and said, "Jesus is gone from the tomb! I don't know where he is!" They ran and looked too, but they didn't know what to do.

Mary was so confused. She stood near the tomb crying. Suddenly, Jesus was standing near her, but she didn't know who he was. He said to her, "Why are you crying? Who are you looking for?"

Mary thought he was the gardener. She said, "Sir, please tell me where you put Jesus."

Then Jesus said her name, "Mary."

When he said her name, Mary realized it was Jesus! She recognized his voice! She was so happy and excited again. Show me your happy puppet and make it jump up and down to show how happy Mary was. She was so happy that she ran and told all the others that Jesus was alive again. He really was God!

Say: **When Jesus rose from the dead, he proved to everyone that he is God. Nobody can do that, but Jesus did! His friends were so happy that he was alive again! They were happy to know he was God. Let's celebrate that Jesus is God.**

Have children set their tomb cups and stones at the table with the smiley side of the stones showing. Show them how to insert a puppet stick into the slit on the bottom of the cup to use as a puppet holder.

Say: **Nothing could hold Jesus down! Not his enemies, not death, not even that big, heavy stone. Let's play a game and be like that stone. Lie on the floor, and roll up like a ball. I'll tell you some great things that Jesus does. Then roll to a new spot, and say, "Jesus is God!" to show that nothing can hold Jesus back.**

Make statements such as the following, giving children time to respond in between. While you play the game, have an adult helper slip a cookie or other special treat under each child's cup without being seen.

- **Jesus walked on water.**
- **Jesus made the wind and waves obey him.**
- **Jesus loves you.**
- **Jesus knows all about you.**
- **Jesus rose from the dead.**

After the last roll, have children go back to the table, and tell them there are surprises inside their tombs. As they eat their treat, remind them that when Mary and her friends looked in the tomb, they too were surprised because Jesus was alive again.

Encourage them to use their puppets, cups, and stones to tell the story of the Resurrection at home to their families.

Talk About It

Ask:

- **What happened to Jesus?**
- **What did Mary see when she looked into the tomb?**
- **How did Jesus' friends know he was God?**
- **How do you know Jesus is God?**

Power Prayer

Jesus, we praise you because you are God. You rose from the dead to prove it. We want to love you and praise you always. Thank you that you are more powerful than anything. We love you, Jesus.

Group Publishing, Inc.
Attention: Product Development
P.O. Box 481
Loveland, CO 80539
Fax: (970) 679-4370

Evaluation for
Make and Play Puppets

Please help Group Publishing, Inc. continue to provide innovative and useful resources for ministry. Please take a moment to fill out this evaluation and mail or fax it to us. Thanks!

● ● ●

1. As a whole, this book has been (circle one)

not very helpful   very helpful

1   2   3   4   5   6   7   8   9   10

2. The best things about this book:

3. Ways this book could be improved:

4. Things I will change because of this book:

5. Other books I'd like to see Group publish in the future:

6. Would you be interested in field-testing future Group products and giving us your feedback? If so, please fill in the information below:

Name _____

Church Name _____

Denomination _____ Church Size _____

Church Address _____

City _____ State _____ ZIP _____

Church Phone _____

E-mail _____

TEACH YOUR PRESCHOOLERS AS JESUS TAUGHT WITH GROUP'S *HANDS-ON BIBLE CURRICULUM*™

Hands-On Bible Curriculum™ **for preschoolers** helps your preschoolers learn the way they learn best—by touching, exploring, and discovering. With active learning, preschoolers love learning about the Bible, and they really remember what they learn.

Because small children learn best through repetition, Preschoolers and Pre-K & K will learn one important point per lesson, and Toddlers & 2s will learn one point each month with **Hands-On Bible Curriculum**. These important lessons will stick with them and comfort them during their daily lives.

The **Learning Lab®** is packed with age-appropriate learning tools for fun, faith-building lessons. Toddlers & 2s explore big **Interactive StoryBoards**™ with enticing textures that toddlers love to touch—like sandpaper for earth, cotton for clouds, and blue cellophane for water. While they hear the Bible story, children also *touch* the Bible story. And they learn. **Bible Big Books**™ captivate Preschoolers and Pre-K & K while teaching them important Bible lessons. With **Jumbo Bible Puzzles**™ and involving **Learning Mats**™, your children will see, touch, and explore their Bible stories. Each quarter there's a brand new collection of supplies to keep your lessons fresh and involving.

Fuzzy, age-appropriate hand puppets are also available to add to the learning experience. What better way to teach your class than with the help of an attention-getting teaching assistant? These child-friendly puppets help you teach each lesson with scripts provided in the **Teacher Guide**. Plus, your children will enjoy teaching the puppets what they learn. Cuddles the Lamb, Whiskers the Mouse, and Pockets the Kangaroo turn each lesson into an interactive and entertaining learning experience.

Just order one **Learning Lab** and one **Teacher Guide** for each age level, add a few common classroom supplies, and presto—you have everything you need to inspire and build faith in your children. For more interactive fun, introduce your children to the age-appropriate puppet who will be your teaching assistant and their friend. No student books are required!

Hands-On Bible Curriculum is also available for elementary grades.

Order today from your local Christian bookstore, or write: Group Publishing, P.O. Box 485, Loveland, CO 80539.

Ministry Resources for Preschoolers!

Pray & Play Bible for Young Children

This Bible story and activity book is certain to become a classic! 14 favorite Bible stories are beautifully bound in a large 9x12 hardcover complete with 4-color artwork throughout. The child-friendly language makes it perfect for your church nursery and preschool classes. This is a memory-making activity book—with 3 pages of activities, snacks, games, crafts, and songs after each story! Children experience and remember each important Bible story!

ISBN 0-7644-2024-0

Wiggly, Giggly Bible Stories About Jesus

Delight your preschoolers with 25 foundational Bible stories from Jesus' life! You actually get 100 stories…because each of the 25 key stories features 4 distinct techniques for telling it! They will love hearing these stories as you wrap Bible truths in finger plays, fun rhymes, motion songs, creative sound effects, puppet plays, and more! Use these flexible 5- to 10-minute stories to extend your teaching time…to jazz up other lessons…any time you want to focus your preschoolers on who Jesus is!

ISBN 0-7644-2046-1

W*O*W! Exploring God's World of Wonder With Preschoolers

Preschoolers *love* to explore and with this kid-friendly guide you'll help children discover God's natural world. You'll connect kids with their Creator through memorable Bible verses, amazing science tricks, motion games, tasty cooking, fun music, stories, and other great activities. This book is for every preschool teacher— especially those who teach Sunday school, children's church, or midweek programs.

ISBN 0-7644-2107-7

My God Is So Great!: 62 Games to Help Preschoolers Know and Love God

Help your preschoolers explore 10 of God's characteristics with games, songs, creative prayers, and other preschool pleasers! Your children will learn to know and love their Heavenly Father as they discover God is all-knowing, creative, loving, forgiving, giving, faithful, powerful, a King…and that God is listening and everywhere. BONUS: Each activity includes age-level insights about how to work with preschoolers and/or ideas to make a great activity even better!

ISBN 0-7644-2094-1

Discover our full line of children's, youth, and adult ministry resources at your local Christian bookstore, or write: Group Publishing, P.O. Box 485, Loveland, CO 80539. www.grouppublishing.com

Welcome to FW Friends™! A revolutionary approach to children's programs.

Get your elementary and preschool kids excited about their Christian faith with FW Friends™! It's the only midweek program that draws kids closer to God by building stronger relationships—with God, their peers, and mentoring adults—through the power of small groups. You can use FW Friends as a midweek program or for Sunday school, an after-school program, or anywhere you want kids to grow closer to God. Everything in FW Friends is designed to help kids know, love, and follow Jesus.

Everything about FW Friends emphasizes lasting spiritual growth. After gathering with their families for a meal, kids go to the Opening Celebration, separate to join their Circle of Friends as they rotate through Discovery Centers, take time for quiet reflection with their journals, then rejoin the other groups for the Closing Celebration.

FW Friends is easy and flexible. Every lesson and activity is clearly and visually laid out in several handy See-It Do-It™ leader guides. Any leader can actually sit down with a group of kids—See-It Do-It guide in hand—and lead them through any activity...with very little preparation needed!

FW stands for FaithWeaver™ and FW Friends is part of the FaithWeaver family of Christian growth resources. Contact us for more information about this family of resources that ties together Bible curriculum, children's church, midweek programming, and the home. FaithWeaver builds on the power of the family to encourage Christian growth.